'OWER DELIBERATIONS' (2021)

(The Saga of Tooting Richard).

by

Atlas D'four.

Dear Reader,

The following narrative evolved from a series of accounts written in the 1970s, then hidden away in a drawer for over thirty years and resurrected in 2000 and again in 2020. The original manuscripts were penned in a burning desire to be brutally honest with oneself and with a desire to encapsulate the memories before time began its insidious pastime of erasing the majority of them and decorating those remaining with a 'rose tinted hue'.

There are many forms of 'truth', i.e. that which the conscious mind accepts and then that which the sub-conscious knows to be the case and buries deep down because of its supposedly unpalatable nature. However. If we as individuals are ever to be our true selves, the first requirement is to accept who and what we are, regardless of the end product.

We are told, we are, each one of us, a product of our genes and our upbringing. A prisoner of our own experiences and memories.

What we delighted in or suffered under, has made us what we have become today, a fact, which because of our youthful vulnerability, we were then powerless to control. We are what our fellow man has made us – Which *should* be a *warning* to us all.

It is incumbent upon me as the author to issue the following *Reader's Health warning :-*

Persons of tender sensibilities or of a delicate nature should *NOT* read the following narrative.

Parents with children under the age of *ten* should avoid this material coming into possession of their offspring, as it may confuse an otherwise stable upbringing.

Atlas D'four. 2021. 'Ower Kid' series. Book 5.

It's 40 years since last we met. (1980)

One's hair was then faux-blonde and set.

It's greyer now but we don't fret.

That's life – as many will find.

For those who are not familiar with my previous ramblings – a list is hereby offered:-

'Ower Kid' Series.   (Bildungs-sach-bucher).

(Autobiographical). (Chronological order).

Ower Darkling

978-1-84944-041-7   (1999)

(Re-issued with changes. UkUnpublished 2010).

Ower Dawning

978-1-84944-054-7   Ditto.

Ower Detinue

978-1-84944-055-4   Ditto.

Ower Dabbling

978-1-84944-056-1   Ditto.

Ower Deliberations (2021). Amazon.

978-1-51479-877-5

The Author – 1995.

That's what 40 years away from home does to you – Another country. A different world. But people never change - - - - or do they?

'Ruination by cheap Chinese labour'.

A 19th century quote. And the world holds its breath. It's the only way to avoid a choking death from the 'wing of bat' – or so we are led to believe. Covid 19. One of many hundreds of corona viruses having escaped the clutches of its host to descend upon silent invisible wings on a culpable human species whose intent is to ultimately destroy their hosts for pecuniary gain. Such arrogance. Akin almost to the arrogance of its intended victims - - - Let battle commence.

We are in the 20th year of our Lord of the 21st century. We have left behind the death and destruction of the century of our birth with all its mindless, callous selfish ways in the hope of better things to come. Dream on Horatio - - .

'He hath awakened from the dream of life. T'is we, who lost in stormy visions keep with phantoms an unprofitable strife and in mad trance strike with our spirits knife invulnerable nothings'. P.B.Shelley 1792-1822.

But I digress from intent. From the industrial township, where even the house sparrows awake each morning coughing, a new horizon awaits. A casting off of the old shackles. We begin the chase. A new country beckons -.

'1981'.

'The Little House on the Hill'.

Contrary to my great expectations my arrival in this green and pleasant lands wasn't heralded from the hilltops nor whispered from the valleys, more muttered from behind steaming foul stinking middens, "For God's sake. What next"? "Is it human"? As the locals watched as I conveyed my many belongings, including a wife and young blonde-haired daughter together with two horses along the short grass filled lane to our new abode. " Well - -. This is it". I announced proudly, in an attempt to accentuate the wisdom of my purchase, sweeping an arm along the full expanse of the wide valley that had opened out before us with its fast flowing river at its base and trying at the same time to ignore the drone of ten million black flies that had suddenly sensed new meat had unexpectedly arrived amongst them and maybe meal time had come early.

The house, only recently built, was square and just the one storey with a roof of ample slope wherein I planned to ensconce myself and my numerous hand-written manuscripts in the hope of isolation and peaceful repose for my forthcoming retirement.

"Yer only thrirty-seven!" growled the Old Lady. "Don't yer think yer should do some work first."

In truth the growl was less than malicious for of her two offspring I had been far, far the more industrious than Ower Kid and most of my contemporary's to date. In fact from the age of ten years old without ceasing. My temporary working hours had always exceeded my schooling hours, when I actually attended school that is, a fact which suited my desires to control my own destiny and which regularly brought me into conflict with all my peers. ("Headmaster. I have a boy who is thinking for himself." "What! Thinking for himself? Have you tried flogging him?") And thus when I muted my desire to leave my home town and shortly thereafter confirmed it, the Old Lady just assumed I was 'running away' again even though the last time, in her mind, had been some 20 years previously. – (See – Ower Dawning).

'Park A Van'. The name of the property. When I first heard it I had assumed perhaps it was just that, a van parked on a field. The price seemed to confirm the description in my minds eye it being sixty percent lower than any appreciable property of my home town of five acres and a dwelling place. So my relief on first sight at the sign on the gate reading 'Parc-Y-Farn', the three sloping meadows to the river, the stable block, caravan and a conglomeration of wooden outbuilding surrounding the 'house on the hill'. Perhaps my luck was in for a change.

Having divested myself of almost everything of material wealth I possessed before leaving ower northern town, the building and developments firms, the taxi firms, the theatrical agency, the quick dabble at my own butchers shop and the property firm, I was left with what I considered was a fair exchange. A family, some livestock and jobless, not that being devoid of actual paying work had any priority, with a yearning to 'start again' perhaps in a year or two if the mood took me. Meanwhile it was going to be 'the good life'. The flora and fauna beckoned. Nature in all its abundance called out to me. "I'm here. I'm here. I'm here." – And boyo, was it here indeed.

The main road had disappeared. A deep mountain of snow covered everything as far as the eye could see broken only by a black winding band snaking across its frozen back, unable as it had been to freeze up the whole width of the river completely. This was the fifth day and still not a single thing across the whole county was, as yet, moving.

"Can I go to school Daddy?"

"Certainly sweetheart. I'll just hitch up the dog team and wax the sledge runners."

When the estate agent said, "It's always that touch warmer across these valleys – it's the Gulf Stream you see - blows warm air so it does." He failed to add – 'sometimes'.

It didn't make any sense at the time. Whereas it does now. When Ower northern town became snow-bound, which it did at least once a year, none of the schools shut or, God forbid, any of the town's business. No buses or cars because the roads were blocked, you walked. More than half an hour late and your pay was docked. No excuses. Advice was in abundance. 'Bad weather – yer need yer big coat lad'. But here in these rural climes it seemed 'hibernation for the duration' was the order of the day and woe betide 'them's whose hasn't gathered their nuts in May' in the sunnier times. And to boot the electric also failed – without fail. "T'is the line down boyo – somewhere." "Well can't they use another one?" - - - "What other one?" To add insult to injury there was no gas either. Although the largest Natural Gas Terminal on the Irish Sea coast was but 50 miles away there was no gas available anywhere within a thirty mile radius – and there still isn't 40 years later. Talk about Swiss Family Robinson – and although Friday came once a week there was no help there either. There was nothing for it. Logs ---.

Taking my trusty axe I trudged through the deep snow towards the tree-line which bordered the small spring on the bottom field. I had forgotten the stream was there. I found it or to be more precise, it found me. Even after my time in the Merchant Navy I still wasn't that keen on ice cold water. - - Not a good day - - .

Before leaving the 'old' country it is true to say I had been obliged to consider what was happening in the town and, as events were to prove, what was happening elsewhere in the world. Nationally the '70's', unlike its previous decade, had proven to be the dregs of those Bacchanalian ecstasies as Glam Rock glittered out the days of 'Flower Power' and the changes so gratefully awaited and experienced gave way to a souring of industrial strives and sadly disappointing enterprise. The new kids on the block wanted treasures without effort and their masters weren't for sharing. A recipe for disaster awaited all concerned – and I had no desires to be part of it. Hence when push came to shove I ferreted out the nearest Bureau of Unemployment, filled out the bible-thick book of forms, and sat back to await the results. - - They weren't long in coming.

I gave the voice on the other end of the telephone the reference number quoted on the correspondence.

"Yes. Thank you. Would you like we undertake this conversation in Welsh?"

"Er - !" Having given my greeting in English and the long drawn out reference number likewise, the question now posed seemed quite pointless. Or is it just me? According to the Old Lady I could be annoyingly awkward at times.

"Er-. Perhaps not thank you very much."

"Duw. Duw. Thank you. There's lovely," said the voice. " For training purposes this conversation is now being recorded, --- in English ---- How can I help you?"

The reason for my enquiry was that a cheque had arrived in my name for many hundreds of pounds. In fact eight times in excess of what I had expected. Being a true believer in democracy and capitalism I immediately thought stupidity and bungling and civil servants of lesser quality and usage than chocolate tea-pots . Apparently I was wrong. It was the correct amount. An easy mistake on my part not being attuned in any respects with the 'welfare state', and certainly not such lavish amounts. I didn't need the money and was about to more or less intimated such to the voice.

"Oh. I see. I was going to return the cheque -." My words created a short pause - - . Then.

"Duw. Duw. You can't do that. No. No. It's the computer you see. Doesn't do cheque-backs. Duw, duw. No. That will never do bach. It's a new computer. Can't handle it you see."

"So what do I do with it?" There was a pause.

"Well you puts it in your bank. I will make a correction and the computer will do the rest. It will shutterrr out and rreadjust and rreplace the overpayment, if there was one."

"I see - - and - - if there wasn't one?"

"One what?" - - "Overpayment." - - I listened at what was a long drawn out breath and the virtual tick-tocking of a mind going into panic.

"Duw, duw. That's not my department bach."

And so it was I was to spend the next two years on welfare cheques, money I didn't need but which was compulsory to cover National Insurance and Pension payments and which eventually depleted in value to something just above subsistence level - as I pondered deeply my adequately filled ongoing retirement. So adequately I began to wonder how I might find the time to go to work should that unlikely event arise and so unlikely the locals on occasion had 'Got a Job' parties to celebrate such small miracles.

'1982'.

'Tooting Richard' Part 1.

Decisions, decisions. Sometimes glad,
sometimes sad. Often ambiguous.

'Opposite the Railway Inn'. I pulled up before the pub's square of rustic picnic tables and stared across at the gates. My eyes moved slowly along the white painted paling's and then up to where a sign was fixed to the rusted corrugated tin sheeting of the wall. It read: 'Rheilfordd Dyfryn' which in my mind could have meant 'Sleepy Glade Lunatic Asylum' as I hadn't a clue as to its real meaning. Almost certainly 'Welsh' like most other things around here and totally undecipherable to anyone east of 'Offa's Dyke'. Still, this was the place according to the directions I had been given.

Leaving my vehicle I crossed over the road. Each step moving ever more cautiously than the one before. I almost slid unwillingly to a halt and peered over the gate. Beyond was a field. Not your usual field. This one seemed to have upset somebody. To my immediate left was the skeleton of a barn. Half constructed breeze block walls, rusting steel girders, devoid of a frontage and the rest topped off with yet more rusting semi-circular tin sheets. Further down stood a pale white caravan and next to that a garden shed built of concrete panels with an asbestos roof that had seen better days. On my right and perched upon what appeared to be a raised plateau edged by a brittle grey canal-type wall was a cattle truck, the kind one might see in a 1940s war film- but without its wheels. Beyond that another caravan, dark green and perhaps twenty feet long and then a collection of strange looking machines that could have possibly originated from one of H.G. Wells fantasy novels - 'Journey to the centre of the mother-in-law' - that sort of thing. Pressed tightly in-between this display of 'allotment type' housings and funnelling out to borders of infinity the dry waist-high grass and brambles showed signs of having been beating back by the passage of human habitation. Deep tracks led off towards what might have been secluded places of welcoming sanctuary. But who knows? Only the very brave or utterly foolish would venture forth into such a wilderness without the benefit of guides and a team of Tibctan Sherpa's. I wasn't very brave - but that didn't stop mc from - 'going in'.

I should have known what foolishness had brought me to this when I opened the gate which promptly fell over backwards down the whole of its length flattening twenty square yards of bramble as it crashed to the ground. Suddenly a face appeared from around the edge of one of the breeze block walls. It was male, around sixty years of age and covered by a huge fuzzy grey/black beard. A woollen bobble cap topped a man's head.

"Duw, Duw. We don't use that you know. T'isn't no good." the man said - in English.

I looked down at the gate, now in various states of disrepair. He was correct. It certainly wasn't. Not now.

Utilising those parts of the gate which seemed capable of taking my weight I ventured towards him. He was perhaps a few inches smaller than me. Definitely broader - but then so is everyone else I have ever come across - and he was wearing a brown coat, the kind worn by grocers and people in the 'shop trade'. As there didn't appear to be any market stalls or semblance of a shop hereabouts I decided he was perhaps 'local' or an eccentric who having been surveying some of the areas 'drover trails' had become disorientated and fallen foul of his bearings. Neither as it turned out was the case. From my new stance those few yards into the field I could see to the far tree line. Above on my left was a large iron bridge with stone abutments on grey shale walls and way off in the distance another bridge but whose access thereto was totally blocked by a forest of thin willow like saplings. I had learned from my few forays amongst the valleys and hills of this, my recently adopted habitat, not to put great trust in the 'locals' when soliciting directions. A Welsh mile more often than not representing five of our English ones and 'straight on' meaning any one of the five roads leading off at the next junction. I decided to double check my bearings.

"Hellan Railway? I was told it was around here somewhere?" The man looked me up and down.

"Duw, Duw. Looks as if you've found it, isn' it. Them's railway gates you be standing on."

It wasn't the answer I had been hoping for. My heart sank. I decided to try again.

"No. Railway. You know. Railway tracks. Engines. That sort of thing. They said it was in this area somewhere. Next to the village?" The man purposely cocked his head to one side. It was either that or his neck muscles had got fed up of holding aloft his aged head and decided to take a rest?

"Yes. Railway. There's a track over there. Just passed the engine shed." he replied pointing in the direction of the concrete garden shed.

"That's an engine shed???"

The man's head snapped back in place. "Yes I know. I should do. I built it. Would you like to see it bach -?"

I didn't reply. I was still trying to decide if the man was indeed missing from one of the local nursing homes or my scant knowledge of 'railways' was indeed that 'scant'!

It was the 'track' that gave it away. Running from behind the shed doors and out across the field for about fifty yards where it stopped unceremoniously up against a bramble bush. Coming from a chequered background of civil engineering and building works I spotted at once the 'track' was much smaller than I had envisaged. My second surprise came with the size of the engine. It was certainly bigger than I expected.

From the size of the track I was thinking 'miniature'. The last time I had seen a miniature steam engine the driver sitting astride it was four times bigger than the poor little thing beneath him. Had it not been that the engine was known as an inanimate object I would have had him arrested on the spot for physical abuse.

"Alan George." said the man smiling.

I smiled back. "Oh right. Pleased to meet you Alan." I said holding out my hand.

The man gave me a look. "Not me boyo. The Engine. She's called Alan. Alan George."

"Oh!" I was a little non-plussed. " Er. Why is 'she' called 'Alan'?" I asked.

The man sighed heavily. It was obviously not the first time the question had been broached.

"Because they ran out of names like 'Thomas' and 'Ivor' and 'Blodwyn'." he replied, probably wishing he had never suggested showing it to me in the first place.

"They call me 'Tom Whiskers'." he grinned ruffling his fingers through his beard a wicked twinkling appearing at the corners of his eyes. I nodded. They would wouldn't they?

"Yes. Very good." I replied stepping away so he could close the doors again. "Who are they?"

"Eh? Oh! The others. The members you know. The society." My ears fluttered. A danger warning.

"Society -??" I ventured cautiously.

Now it wasn't that I didn't know what a 'society' was. We had one or two of them back home. Co-Operative Society. The Pioneers Society. They ran grocers shops. Perhaps that was why he was wearing the brown coat? Him being a member of a society. Stands to reason.

"Yes. The railway. It's a society you see. Run for the benefit of its members. I'm the chairman of the 'committee'." Oh dear. Committee! I had heard about 'committee's. We had hundreds of them where I came from. Mainly in 'Working Men's Clubs'. This wasn't sounding too good.

When asked by the spokesman representing the inhabitants of a hamlet near my home town - why the new statue in the park had the Duke of Wellington sitting astride a camel and not a horse? The Mayor - representing the council, replied the work had been commissioned by the Ways and Means Committee. Apparently that seemed to satisfy the 'press' and everyone else? The 'Duke' still sits astride his camel to this very day.

But I digress -.

Together we stumbled back the way we had come. Parts of machinery and large lumps of rotting timbers threatened to remove what skin there was affording protection to my lower limbs.

"Why have you got a railway in the middle of a field?" I asked side slipping my thighs away from the blades of a large fan unit minus its grill.

"Field?" For a moment the man seemed unsure of the question then - "Duw, Duw. S'not a field. If it was a field we would have sheep on it. This is Wales you know boyo. No, no. This is the station yard man. It just wants a spot of clearing doesn't it. A few weeds. The odd bramble. Nothing to get excited about bach. Er - -." The man's eyes narrowed. "Er - I don't suppose you have a lawn mower in that van of yours do you?" he smiled. I hadn't. He seemed disappointed. Still. I had to admire his spirit. A combined harvester would have taken the best part of a day to remove the waist high grass had it been able to negotiate amongst all the detritus hidden half submerged in the undergrowth.

"Are you interested in railways then?" he asked as we reached the two tall wrought-iron gate posts that indicated the railway entrance.

"Er. No. Not really. But thanks for showing me your engine."

The man scratched at his whiskers. "Dim problem. Close the gate on your way out." He smiled and disappeared back behind his breeze block wall.

"Close the - - ." What gate? There was nothing left of the gate. Certainly nothing that would 'hang' together. Is that what passed for humour in this neck of the woods?

I paused in the centre of the road and read the sign again. No. Nothing. The 'words' were as much a mystery to me as what had transpired in the last fifteen minutes. I almost retraced my steps in a bid to ascertain the man had 'actually' been there and that it wasn't just a hallucination of sorts. I promised myself to check out the vegetable rack upon my return home. Those mushrooms the wife said she had picked -. I've heard about Welsh mushrooms let me tell you.

One thing was for sure. Tomorrow I would be telephoning the 'Job Agency' and making a few checks. My C.V. stated 'Contracts Manager'. Civil Engineering and Building. Not - 'Variety Act Magician'.

I started the van's engine and as an afterthought looked over my shoulder. No. I didn't have the lawn mower in amongst my plethora of building tools. It had been known. I gave the 'sign' another glance. I wouldn't be seeing it again I thought. Huh -. Little did I know -.

'Allan George' locomotive – crinkling along her track'.

'Between cultures'.

We are in the era of the 'Iron Maiden'. Those years of one Margaret Thatcher and the dismantling of Britain's massive dirty and soul destroying industrial past. A time of renewal. A new horizon of 21st century technology beckons and of service industries and global aspirations. But first we must shed those traditional pastimes and cultural encumbrances that cling to the country's fabric like peanut butter to one's nether parts. Out with the old. In with the new. – Only no-one had informed that part of the British workforce who still lived in the 19th century and still cherished their flat caps, their strong ale and regularly beat the wife in preference to their whippets. 'Some things that doesn't mess wi', was the cry as they reached for their 'big coats' and 'brass studded dog leads'. The fight was on.

'Orgreave'. A British Steel coking works in South Yorkshire, England and a name that sends shudders down the backs of any Whitehall government and left-wing socialist striker.

The why's and wherefore's to tell of that macabre social unrest would take up the rest of my story, but safe to say 'it was a battle of who rules' – government or unions and who would ultimately win. The government won of course. But not before utilising the most nefarious methods of undercover agents, dirty money and the most callous of tactics imaginable. It pleased the rest of the nation's populace. 'In place of strife', a government catch-phrase of the time. 'Winters of discontent'. 'Three-day weeks'. 'Rampant Inflation', and to cap it all 'Britain-The Sick man of Europe', was quite enough for one decade. It was time for a change. Time to move on. Time to finally drop the cobwebbed trappings of 'Empire' and its grubby slavish industrial past. The Iron Maiden was polishing her burnished shield and reflecting the dazzling sun's rays towards a new bright horizon. A New Britain for a New Decade. 'Onward Britannia'. 'Onward'.

'And it came upon a morning clear'. Twenty one. The final count. "Shall we give it another half an hour?" My request came in the form of a question.

"Duw, Duw. If we do that t'will be time for lunch."
"No,no bach. I think we should make a start before some of them think we was just joking and begin to wander off."

Uncomprehendingly I am standing inside the dark green caravan overlooking the bramble-strewn yard amongst a gathering of humanity the likes of which would have struck abject fear into a convention of 'berserkers' or a gathering of 'lesbian rights protestors'. We are here to build a 'railway'. Yes dear reader. You got it in one – a railway. It wasn't to start anywhere. It wasn't to go anywhere. It was just to – be – or not - as the case - may be.

"Is there actually a point to it?" I had asked at the time.

"Well -." The woman in the hippy-styled flower arrangement that was passing for a frock said -, "It's to fulfil the members dream and to satisfy the £90,000 we have secured as a grant for the works and to reduce the unemployment figures for the area."

I frowned and nodded sagely. Apparently that was what one did when dealing with public officialdom in these parts. "I see." I replied. – I didn't but I doubt it would have made the slightest iota of a difference.

I dubbed them – 'Ye motley folorn crew'. For they were. Ranging from 16 years old and just out of school to three of middle-age and one falling over on the verge of retirement. Either that or he had had a very hard life. Twenty one hand-picked unemployed hard-cases, many having not worked a day in their lives and with no intention of ever doing so – if they could help it. I decided it was best to make an impression. Setting fire to the caravan seemed a good idea at the time and calling it a draw. It was only a fleeting thought – fortunately.

It was yet another of the Thatcher years solutions to reduce the unemployment figures, then standing at over three million, and to give the impression that 'government cared'. It didn't, but what the hell. The Manpower Services Commission. A grand title for a massive form of money wasting on temporary projects ranging from Cockle Picking in the Outer Hebrides to Basket Weaving on the lower Severn and various mind-blowing schemes in-between. All relied on government grants and all relied on a willing band of volunteers to instigate such and, when the paid workers had departed having paid lip-service to poor practices, those same volunteers were meant to up keep the resulting semi-skilled devastation. In truth a 'smoke-screen' to cover over the destruction of whole communities whose life-styles had been lost with their glorious industrial pasts. 'In place of strife' it may have been, but it was doing nothing for my sanity as I embarked upon a new phase of 'life' - - - but not as I had known it let me tell you. Talk about lessons in the learning! 'Duw, duw'.

I can truthfully report it took all of three months just to instil in them the habit of getting out of bed and arriving on site every working day -. "Every day"? "What. You mean one day after another?" Barrackroom had asked scathingly. I called him that because he seemed to think he had the qualified answer to every question posed amongst the group. "Yes. Every day. Starting Monday and ending Friday". I held my breath awaiting the pearl of wisdom that I knew was coming. "Er – is that in our contracts then"?

And a further three months to instil a 'work ethic'.

Coming from the private sector and mainly from my own private ownership my advancing into the 'public sector' was akin, I imagine, to having to be reborn. Talk about 'lifting a veil' – more like an 'Iron Curtain'.

And for that I needed my own 'Iron Lady'.

'Somebody lost twenty years'.

"Nine bloody hours." "Nine," snapped the Old Lady. "
It took mi less time t' get through the Manchester
'Blitz' in forty-one – nine hours-." She wasn't pleased.
Nothing new there then. I looked at the Old Man. I
could have parroted his reply with hesitation. "Aye. Bit
of er trek." Its not that I wasn't pleased to see them
or that they had made the effort. I consoled myself
with the thought their stay would be for less than a
fortnight and then it would take them another nine
hours to return 'up North' from whence we all came.

The 'Beeching' cuts of the '60's' of the rural rail links
had made accessing these balmy areas of the country
nothing short of a nightmare. As the crow flies it was
less than two hundred miles. But as a transit route it
had become a game of snakes and ladders. Down a
bit, across a bit, down a bit, up a bit, in a bit, back a
bit and walk the remainder, had indeed taken all of
the much rebuked nine hours. We were in for a heavy
night – and to make matters worse we didn't have any
whisky or the 'Old Lady's balm' as I called it. Three
glasses of whisky made nice (with water) and she was
quite likely to pole-axe the nearest bloke just for the
hell of it. Not that she probably ever had. But the
'look' she would give was sufficient let me tell you.

Gathering the family and livestock together on our
baggage train and heading south hadn't been a
decision taken lightly. But needs must when the devil
drives. Land and house prices in Northern England had

been rapidly on the rise, especially if both were required together. Ower town, following the demise of the God Cotton, was awash with unemployment and a creeping outburst of civil disorder were a portend of things to come. Another problem, one that did not dare speak its name, was the results of the governments drive for immigrant labour of the 60's and 70's and the upsurge in the divides now becoming apparent across many of the urban districts and a 'ghettoising' of the populations. None of which boded well for everyone concerned. And the times they were a changing.

"No! Top of the lane. Turn right, then left and it's about a mile down on the left-hand side." One wished one had repeated the instructions more succinctly. Not that the Old Lady ever took much notice of what a man might say –' They's alright fer bringing the coal in. But not much use fer owt else'. -.

It was going dark when they both returned, the Old Man half carrying the Old Lady whose left leg seemed to be dragging furrows through my pristine gravel driveway. "Here's yer bloody lettuce." The lettuce surrounded by a plastic carrier bag sliced passed my ear. "Bloody place this is. Middle of bloody nowhere."- "Don't just bloody stand there. Help mi in -."

By turning left instead of right at the top of the lane in order to visit the local 'commune', in order to purchase a lettuce, then they deciding to continue in a circular fashion would bring them back to the right place, they had hiked a distance of almost six miles. Why they had imagined there would be side roads or ginnels for short-cuts in the outlands of wild West Wales one cannot imagine. Whatever, it was not an auspicious start for the one and only visit they would ever make to their adventurous offspring's new abode. For them a large gardened bungalow amongst the satanic empty cotton mills and a bus-stop twenty yards away made much more sense – and yer can keep yer countryside lad sethay. You can take the Northerner out of the North but you can't take the North out of the Northerner. In this case such was true, so very, very true.

"I've seen more shops in a Woolworth's Arcade. Is this it?" A journey some three miles and a visit to our local market town had the Old Lady trying to nod her approval for the wife's benefit. "It get's busier on a Friday." replied the wife. "The farmers come with their livestock and usually fill the place." The Old Lady nodded again swinging her head from side to side. "Wouldn't take many of them would it," she sniffed. In truth she was right, half a dozen land rovers and trailers and the place came to a standstill. "They say they are going to paint some double yellow lines for the parking." the wife offered. "Keep a bit of order." "Parkin'," Again the head began shaking. "Where?"

Meanwhile I had promised the Old Man a day out at the railway - - -. The one you might remember I had been asked to 'build'.

'Going 'round the Bend'.

"No. Not possible. Can't be done. The Railway Inspectorate won't allow it."

So that was that then.

"Why not?" I asked. The young man, who went by the name of 'Richard', fixed me with a look of pity. You could tell he considered me one deprived of the 'knowledge', the knowledge of 'railways and their mysteries', a lesser being and to be treated with extreme care and sympathy.

"Because you cannot have a platform with a bend in it."

I was non-nonplussed. In fact my non had never been so 'plussed' before. "But it's got a bend in it now!" I retorted, scanning the length of the platform my eyes gliding slowly down and around the length of the platform's distinctive curve. Richard smiled, or at least his lips curled. I suppose it could have been a sneer. But what do I know.

I tuned to the boys. "OK. That settles it then. Take it down."

The Hellan platform, just the south side of it, stood nearly four feet high. It was built from grey shale stone cuttings, some of which weighed in at a ton each and was bonded together by a dark grey cinder/mortar bedding but which for all its age and dilapidation had the adhesive properties of high-grade super-glue that required some wizardry and a large machine to separate. We hadn't got a 'machine' or a Welsh wizard, so I distributed three six foot heel bars and three heavy duty sledge hammers for the use of. The 'boys' looked at me dumbfounded as if say "Oh yea and where's Superman and his team of Tibetan Sherpa's then?" Dues due, they did have a point -!

The 'new' platform was to be built west of Hellan bridge in the 'new' cutting. It was to be 150 foot long and at rail level to accommodate for the new type of rail transport which in due course Hellan Station was about to receive. The stones from the original platform would form the rear wall and be built on a slight angle to buttress the earthen bank beyond. Which seems all well and good. But not if your 'labour' has been press-ganged from the local 'don't wannabee's' and haven't worked a day in their lives - at least not legally!

Moving half a platform, for that was the end result, a quarter of a mile in a wheelbarrow, may sound like fun. It wasn't. And with the incessant rain that comes with commencing the works in November it wasn't long before the 'effort' became too much for those 'uninitiated in the ways of manual labour' who promptly found ways of either pretending to work or disappearing into the undergrowth like Mabinogion wood nymphs.

"Duw, duw. It's not done like that boyo. Prrrecision boyo. You need prrrecision."

I looked down by my side at the diminutive figure of Mr Whiskers still wearing his bobble-cap above his round impish like face and his large shaggy beard. For a moment I thought I was hallucinating. Where the heck had he sprung from? Too much black coffee. Then he spoke again. " I was a minor you know." he said. I thought, so was I but you grow out of it don't you? "Worked thirty years down the pit I did. Man and boy so to speak." The 'penny' dropped. Oh. That kind of 'minor'. No wonder he was so small!

"Find the seam. Give it a gentle tap. Then whap it." he ordered.

I looked at what remained of my motley crew and thought. I'd love to whap the bloody lot of them but it's not allowed (this being a 'government' scheme where you couldn't even 'fire' anybody.)

"Here. Let me show you boyo." He was instantly offered the three crow-bars. In fact he was so very nearly killed in the rush as the boys tried desperately to divest themselves of their 'work' tools.

"When I nod my head. You hit it." he said. At that point I called a halt to the proceedings. My 'boys' had a habit of taking things very literally. I didn't want any dead 'minors' on my site, regardless of their age.

"Duw, duw. A bit tough that. Not like anthracite at all." said my diminutive little friend after his sixth attempt to split the stone from its glutinous bindings. I didn't comment. Well you don't do you. He was trying to be helpful. As are most railway volunteers. Instead I smiled and thanked him for his advice and strenuous effort. "Time for a cup of tea I think." he said looking at me expectantly.

"Shhh. For Pete's sake. Don't mention the word 'tea'. They'll think it's going home time." Alas too late. I looked round to find an empty space where my team of 'workers' had been standing. It wasn't all that was standing either. So still was the bloody platform - .

Mr Whiskers had ensconced himself appropriately on a rusting tractor seat that waved disconsolately above the level of brown seeded grasses and dead brambles Bakelite cup in one hand and smouldering pipe in the other. "T'is going to take a while with these boys," he mused waving the pipe stem towards the green caravan, "But your lad here is doing a grand job – so far." The Old Man took a draw on his cigarette. Like me he was probably picturing something he might well have seen in a posh garden back home. Gnome like but more gaily painted. "Supposed to be completed inside twelve months -." he went on, " – more like twelve years at this rate." "A danger in the pit this lot. Duw, duw yes. Couldn't send them down there. Duw, duw no. Got your work cut out with these lad – terrible." The Old Man looked at me and shrugged. "Where there's life there's hope." Mr Whiskers gazed

at him for a time then -."Life - -! They's alive then.?
He did have a point. If money doesn't motivate - - !

Cannabis. Weed. Ganja. Welsh snuff. Row upon row of
it. And in my forest.

For the past few weeks the work had been progressing
at a remarkable rate. The eagerness to rebuild the
perimeter fences, almost three miles in length, was
more than a bit of a surprise. There was an almost
audible groan from those working line-side or in the
yard areas as the 'fencing squads' skipped gaily
passed wheelbarrows squeaking, hand tools rattling
and chatting away ten to the dozen. When Mr
Whiskers volunteered to help, just to inspect the
previous day's works of course, it resembled Walt
Disney's Seven Dwarfs and but for the raucous foul
language might easily have passed as such.

'I li ho. Hi ho, and off to work we go. With shovels and
picks and rolls of tin-foil sticks. Hi ho, hi ho, hi ho, hi
ho, hi ho - and off t' - - - - . Bloody tin-foil - - - ?

As I emerged into the 'glade' the temperature rose a
full ten degrees. The forest floor had been recently
cleared and there across an area at least fifty yards by
fifty yards row upon row of hooped poly-tunnels some
six feet high shimmered in the mid-afternoon's
reflective haze of the weak early Spring sun.
Squatting on an upturned bucket, a spiral of blue-grey
smoke issuing from his beard, sat Barrackroom, a
glazed smile across his features. "Hey up Boss." he
murmured before again sucking on a nine inch long

crudely rolled stick of tobacco and cannabis he had been hiding behind his back as he heard my approach. "What are you doing here?" he asked.

What? What was I doing there? What was he doing there? For a second or two I imagined I had tumbled down a rabbit-hole and emerged into a Lewis Carrol fantasy land. "Me -?" "What am I - - ?" "You are supposed to be with your gang down by the big bridge – fencing." Barrackroom nodded and spun both eyes in opposite directions, an easy trick to do with a brain-full of dope. "Plants -. Needed watering. Won't grow without it -." A pregnant pause ensued then -. "Won't grow --.You're not supposed to be growing bloody plants. You're supposed to be working. You're in charge of a team of men. What do you think would happen if the Railway people found this lot or even heard about it?"- "They won't find it. And they won't know about it unless' somebody tells them will they ?" he countered, nodding his head towards the perimeter of the clearing. "It's not on Railway land." I turned and looked back. Sure enough the clearing began a bare three inches outside the old GWR oak post and wire fencing. The plantation was on someone else's land and consequently very deep inside the neighbours forest where humans hadn't been in almost centuries past. He was right about it not being found – although I had. But in truth I had tracked back from the track-bed where dozens of muddy feet had flattened the winter-burnt undergrowth curious as to why this part of the development was so popular. I think I'd just answered my own question.

'Tinker-Bell cometh'

The laying down of the 'railway' and its environs, originally in the latter 1800's by the Great Western Railway, following numerous attempts by others, and it's consequent closure in 1972 by British Rail, this bold attempt at some dream of renewal had found favour with the powers that be. 'Although don't talk too loud about money it may give the impression we have some. Lay out a twelve month plan and we will marvel at your ingenuity', they said. So they did.

Twelve miles of track-bed and around one hundred and twenty acres. Twenty three bridges ranging from a mini eighty foot viaduct to a stone-laid culvert and twenty four miles of dilapidated oak post fencing with numerous non-existent gates. " But you don't want all that. Never do. Too much worry in one go Bach. Shall we say about this much -?" The Chairman of the Board, a Mr Llewellyn, cupped both hands around the centre of the plans laying on the table and smiled at me. "Just this little bit - - as a starter."

Scheme One. (The railway yard and one mile west.) All services and safety fences. New rail track. One Engine shed. One Carriage shed and Carriage, One ticket office. One toilet block. One renovated coal shed and a Children's Play area. Splendid I thought. "So – and what have we got on site now." A fairly straightforward question one might have thought. I looked around the table at the selection of railway directors, mostly ageing, definitely self-important. A few grimaces, the odd nervous cough and -. "Well. Hmm. Let's see now. There's an electric socket in the little office by the gate and there's a tap in the tool shed and I think there's a few shovels in there as well. Hmmm. Yes. I'm pretty certain we have those." My turn - "And toilets, changing rooms, eating/rest area - - medical stuff - - anything like that maybe -?" The directors looked at me blankly then at each other and finally back at me. "Duw.duw. Don't think so bach. Not toilets - - -but you will be building some of those won't you?" I stared at these known high pinnacle personages of the railway company as a vision of my workforce hopping around clutching at their nether regions and whispering at each passing day – "The bogs will be ready in a month or two. Can't wait. Can't wait." – flashed before my eyes. It was then I well and truly confirmed in my own mind that I had landed feet first, solidly and succinctly feet first, in a world of innocent make-believe. I was passing through a dream where reality no longer existed and where all things were possible if one just wished it to be so. 'Dragons of marzipan, cottages of sponge-cake and 19th century transportable vehicles of marshmallow with candy-floss clouds issuing from under their ginger-bread cloakings'. Now I know where Lewis Carol got all his ideas from. I thought I had better confirm the extent of the 'contract' just to be in the 'know' because it certainly wasn't to be 'safe'. "It is supposed to be a twelve month scheme isn't it." "Er – oh indeed bach. Do you think that is too short? Perhaps - - you could stretch it out a bit –?" - - - -

Meanwhile out in the real world. Away from dreams of 'steam'. In a world where man must strive or die and opportunities must be grasped with both hands I came across a friend of Peter Pan's. However, I wasn't putting my hands in that pile of horse dung just so this Welsh fairy could prove his point. - - "You demolish a knackered wardrobe, made of oak you see. You take the stout pieces and you bury them in the horse shit. You leave them there for four to five years and then you retrieve them. Today is retrieval day. You want 16th century oak -," he grinned. "Help yourself boyo." To understand any of this we must retreat a little to my first year in our new home when meeting the locals seemed a good idea at the time. A visit to town – I say town but by northern standards it would barely have constituted a small Lancashire village – on a Friday. Market day. When all the surrounding farmers descend to this one focal point with their livestock, park anywhere, divest themselves of the stock and their hermit-like predilections, drink copious gallons of strong ale and make derogatory remarks regarding the townsfolk, the tourists, the English, the local council and the price of anything and everything before returning whence they came leaving streams of animal effluence over almost everything in sight. It was amongst these milling gatherings I met one Lionel Braveheart, a lean little fellow, similar to myself but he looked healthier (then again most people do) and a smile that looked welcoming amongst the dour, darkened features of these other natives of late. He was into 'antiques, well not so much 'antiques' as younger antiques. Yes. I know. You will say there are no such things. So will I. But you're now in Wild West Wales and things are different here and if they are not, they strive to make them so. Boyo.

It is auction day at the small market town of Lampeter, which as few will know is in Ceredigion. Yes. I know I couldn't pronounce it either. It's a Tuesday. Each day of the week has a purpose including Sunday which is Chapel Day. Our new 17th century Welsh dresser is about to stand the scrutiny of narrowed, piercing dark eyeballs as they prod and probe and fingers caress the well worn almost black patina of the highly polished oak boards.

"Stuart is it?" asked the prospective bidder.

"No. It's Lionel. Have we met?" replied my illustrious friend.

"Duw, duw no. I don't think so. I mean Stuart is it? Charles Second. Jacobean perhaps?"

Lionel wasn't going to be caught out so easily. It's a criminal offence to knowingly sell a product under a false provenance. "That's a difficult one. It's of that style as you can see. But if it is it will be one of a very few that escaped the fire." "It's been in a fire?" "No. Not recently. The Great Fire. London 1666. It wouldn't be here had it been there - at the time."

In truth it had. Been in a fire. I know. I'd spent the best part of two days with a blow-torch 'patining' the plate shelves to get them to the right colour.

"Ooo. Yes. No. I see. Hmm. Lovely isn't it."

It auctioned off for two hundred and fifty pounds. Had it have been 'Stuart' or 'Jacobean' the figure would have been ten times that. Today it stands in a Welsh cottage in St Fagin's Welsh Life Museum quite proudly labelled 'Original 17thc Open-backed Welsh Dresser'. But it isn't. It's a horse poo soaked Victorian wardrobe lovingly tended by a master craftsman from London made to look like an original artefact from a bygone age and passed through half a dozen hands, each raising the price, until finally falling into the hands of 'experts' - - -. And at that point I rest my case.

Tinkerbell was the local supplier of everything and anything. Being local what he didn't know of the area could be written on the back of a postage stamp. If you wanted a stand-alone Victorian apple corer Tinkerbell was your man. If he didn't know, then he knew a man who did- who also knew a man who did. The 'ring' went by the name of the 'valley mafia' and like their name sake weren't timid about getting what they wanted. To cross them or make them loose face one needed to be prepared to 'move' shortly thereafter. In truth they were vital in these parts to getting things done.

Lionel knew these people, having been in the valley some years and requiring some of their 'special services'. I knew Lionel, which put me in the loop. But I also knew I would have to spend a number of years 'proving', like a bowl of fermenting dough, before I would be 'trusted' and 'brought in' for 'initiation'. 'Well boyo see – you is English - . Isn' it?'

'Welsh Garden'.

If the county of Kent be the 'Garden of England' then without doubt 'Wild West Wales' be the garden of Wales. A small country adjoining the wider girth of England from its ponderous rolling hills to the east, its jagged majestic mountains in the north, its stunted hills and valleys to the south to its sea-lashed beaches and valleys in the west – Wales has a fascinating beauty all of its own. My choice of a long winding, tree massed valley brought back memories of Ower town in the north of England with its surrounding moorlands interspersed with wooded valleys and glittering streams but minus the soot-blackened cottages with their exhausted slate roofs and peeling whitewashed walls – here the birds didn't cough, no dogs ran wild and the rats kept to themselves with a run of endless green countryside in which to forage and wander.

And it was here with a recent influx of immigrants from England that someone suggested the building of a 'tourist trap'. A valley of boundless pleasure for the discerning visitor. A Mecca of delights. - - -. That took a while to sink in let me tell you. "But – but. Does you mean foreigners boyo?" "English people?" "Duw,duw!" "Well there's something isn' it!"

I took a look through the local advertising journal and discovered fifteen woollen mills, a coracle museum and a multitude of craft establishments. Search as I might I could find very little of anything for the under sixties unless one counted a cinema and putting green at the far end of the valley in a local coastal town, certainly nothing that said 'Kiss me quick' or even 'Give us a peck when you've got a minute to spare'. I was however constructing a narrow-gauge railway which with a bit of imagination could entice the 'family' fraternity. So perhaps there was hope where previously there had been a deepening despair. This was a job for Eleanor, she of the hippie flower-patterned frock. What was needed here was university tutored gobbledygook, liberally peppered with a misty haze of impressive statistics, all wrapped up and neatly presented with a brutal but determined undeniable logic only 'one with a degree' could muster. In effect -. A cunning plan - - - .

The addition of the word 'Tourist' pushed the grants up from £75,000 to £95,000 which together with the railway society's own meagre funds and a chip from the company bankers guaranteed a spend of £110,000 for Manpower Services Scheme 1 – A Narrow-Gauge Tourist Railway, a catalyst to ensnare the droves of wandering visitors to the valley and its bountiful delights.

"The only bloody things that have been drove through here is long-horned cattle and goats," growled the taller of the Clancy brothers, the one with the plaster cast having attempted to chain-saw off his big toe in order to avoid digging post-holes, "Couldn't they come up with a place a bit more hidden?"

They do say 'from the mouth of babes the truth shall flow' and in this case it fit the bill, Pembrokeshire being the historical tourism area of West Wales and to where the 'hordes' descended. This was not in Pembrokeshire. It was near. A Welsh near. About 40 miles, as the crow flies. Which in Australian terms is next door. But here on our small island, the size of a pin-head on a large drawing pin, it's like 'miles away' and petrol is part of our gold standard.

Location, location, location! 'Problem number 1'.

It's difficult to put into words (without blaspheming) how ower country, Great Britain, ever became 'Good' never mind 'Great' when it is considered some of the 'minds' that operate it. The main requirement for a 'railway' is - - - 'rail' - - which also cannot function without a solid foundation, ergo - railway 'sleepers'.

The 'rail' arrived on the back of ten tipper wagons and the sleepers on a further 6 flat bed trucks. I drew Mr Whiskers to one side.

"Why is it all concertinaed together?" I asked.

"Well you see. When you buys it. It's in one big pile. Two hundred and fifty tons you see." I couldn't say that answered my question. "Yes. But it's all, well, it's all tangled together. Shouldn't it be, sort of straight, in long lines and crane lifted not - - ". My words were drowned out by a thunderous crashing as two of the huge tipper wagons promptly disgorged their loads of tangled steel in a screeching crescendo into the middle of the yard. " - - not dumped like a pan-load of spaghetti?" - - I continued as the crashing ceased momentarily.

"Duw, duw, S'not new. Second hand it is, Can't afford new. Sleepers are second hand too. Got to sort out the rotten ones. Good for the fire-box. Burn like buggery they does. Whoosh. Brilliant."

MoD Trecwn. Ministry of Defence Ex-Naval Ammunition Base on the west coast of Wales. Second hand, as also the rail spikes and fish-plates and not one piece less than 30 years old if a day. I pointed towards one rail that stood apart from the pile. It seemed possibly straighter than the rest as there were no thirty degree kinks in it. "How do you propose we remove the 'kinks'?" "The kinks?" "Yes. The wiggly bits." Mr Whiskers grinned at me. "Like we does down the mines boyo." He raised both arms to shoulder height. "You bends them back across your neck doesn't you"

I paused, my forefinger securely holding both my lips tightly together. If these were portends of things to come – boy were we in trouble. I glanced across towards the yard gates, now rebuilt and shining white in their new timbers. Should I, or should I not, make a run for them now - - - ?

East or West? The question had hung like a Damocles sword over the ' Railway Society' for nigh on 10 years prompting half the members to leave in a huff for more aesthetic climes and begin another rail project further down the valley and with the residue pondering the viability of it all and – shouldn't they just all go home?

Go West young man. Such may have been true for their Victorian ancestors but highly suspect in the days of 'Maggie Thatcher'. Nevertheless, West it was.

"We hit the bridge two miles down. Then across the river to the town." said Eleanor, she of the flowered patterned frock. "Three miles of beautiful woods and meadowlands – a restful trundle – a rural idyll." 'I really must get this bloody woman to stop basket-weaving in her spare time was the first thought that came to mind'. "So does that mean we will operate from the town eastwards?" I asked. Quite a reasonable assumption on my part. "Well – no, not exactly. You see the track-bed doesn't go into the town. It stops about half a mile away. There is a station yard – but we don't own it." I nodded sagely. One does when dealing with the Welsh Intelligence Service. It was like trying to get blood out of a stone.

"So who does?" I asked. A sweet smile followed by, "Er – Jones the Coal - -!" - - I see. Jones the bloody coal. There must have been at least five 'Jones the Coal' within one square mile of Hellan not to mention similar with Jones the Baker, Jones the Butcher and Jones the mad-cap chapel curator.

"So where does the track-bed end?" I ventured cautiously. Again a pause then. "In the back garden of the Glove Factory."- - No. No. Absolutely not. I was not going there. This conversation had run off its own track and hit the bloody bridge – some two miles down going westward. Surely I must have something better to do? – But - West it was – and one must hope we wouldn't come across a inebriated tribe of Red Indians or any Welsh buffalo herds on the way. – Wanna bet -.

Next on the list. Toilets. A new building, grant assisted – someone had promised they would be always be open to the general public – and thus attracted the interest of the local council who delved into their community chest and extracted around ten percent of the total costs for the use of. It should have been used to import a gang of Polish tradesmen and labourers was my first thought as I asked for bricklayers, plumbers, electricians and joiners to step forward. The joinery foreman Johnnie Greybeard tottered forward. He was sixty years old if a day and looked as if he could just about manage a foot-stool but certainly not a roof. The electrician was at least somewhat younger, RAF trained and looked to all intents and purposes as he might know what he was doing. "A bricklayer?" I ventured hopefully. No one else moved. "Stonemason?" - - - - . Not a quiver. "Anyone ever build a manhole?" A ripple of head movements then a mini chorus of. "Septic tanks!"

"Good. Then you should know how to lay bricks?" "Er – no Boss. Concrete you see. Big rings and a tractor. Farms you see and community dwellings. Got to be big. Lots of shit you see. Big concrete rings and concrete copings. Wooden some of them. But no. No bricks." Ah well. It had been worth a try. So I still needed at least one Polish tradesman. Unsurprisingly

Mr Whiskers knew of one. He was Ukrainian, Boris the Builder from Borth, Ukrainian was near enough. As long as he could lay bricks that was fine by me. He could have been an Inuit from Greenland for all I cared. The urgent needs of proper toilets for the twenty one of us was rapidly becoming a problem. "I have his address. You can give him a bell Bach." A 'bell'! Oh my God. I had a fleeting vision he would probably be blind - - . Yes. I know. But you weren't there -! You should remember I have arrived from civilisation where the electric, telephones and television signals are constantly available. Where gas runs through pipes. Not where Friday means a Friday in a week sometime later in the year. Where you need to put a full day out on one side to find the nearest supermarket. Where people don't constantly remind you that they love a 'challenge' and they call a large round canvas covered garden trug a sea-salmon fishing boat. - Now there really is a challenge - - - - - - ! And so we began to build.

The door to my tiny office opened and a head appeared. "Billy the Kid's gone fell off the wagon Boss." said Barrackroom a crease of a frown overshadowing his black shaggy beard. Billy the Kid so named for his youthful appearance and a propensity to 'rob' anything not nailed down. "I didn't know he drank." I countered. "No he's really come off. He was standing on the end of a rail across one of the sleepers (he didn't mean one of the work-gang – I will leave you to work that one out) and the boys dropped another rail off on the other end. Did a beautiful

somersault he did. Going well it was. Until he landed -
- on his head." Ah well -. Never a day goes by as they
say.

Surprisingly there were few 'accidents' apart from the
odd chain-saw miscalculation or spike hammer aim. It
was mandatory for all to have safety equipment which
included wellingtons, steel-capped boots, sou-wester
oilskins and working gloves. The first batch lasted all
of eight days before calls came in for a re-supply.
Which I duly ordered. The second batch – all of a
fortnight. It wasn't until I questioned the 'usage' that
it came to light that they weren't so much 'lost' or
'used up' but were being 'sold' by some of the boys to
the local farmers at the Friday stalls in the nearby
Mart. At next morning's roll-call I announced a 'block'
on further 'loses' and that new equipment would only
be purchased at quarterly intervals. If I couldn't get in
on it. I was having it stopped. The losses rapidly
reduced. As did those of the shovels, pick-axes, heel
bars and wheelbarrows. If the boys thought by
divesting themselves of working equipment they
wouldn't have to do any, work that is, - how so wrong
they were. Although in truth some of the 'work'
produced by good intent would have sent a good Clerk
of Works into fits of rabid despair. "Why are you
bothering?" asked Barrackroom. "There's nothing to
draw with all this. At the end of the year we are all
sacked. This lot will be back in the hands of their
volunteers who have done virtually buggar-all in the
last ten years and the weeds will return with a
vengeance?" – He had a very good point did the guy.

'The Owd Town'.

(Looks almost the same.)

As the boys considered a Saturday as sacrosanct for the worship of 'rugby' and Sunday for growing 'weed' my departure on the Friday afternoon for the 'old town' would fit in nicely. A four hour journey by road. Three hours to get out of Wales and one hour on a decent motorway, of which most of Wales had none.

The lay-by, on the rise from the three-lane carriageway, exposed the old town in all its fleeting glory. "Yep. – Still there then." Not that such could have been otherwise. I mused with the thought of playing one of ower childhood games of 'Count the tall chimneys' which in those days had numbered some one hundred plus. I stopped at thirty six. Still some way to go to remove the blots on the landscape and a very, very long way to go to make it once again anything worthwhile. 'Maggies' miracles weren't working here – or if they were someone was making a bloody good job of hiding them.

It was dirty. The town had always been dirty but somehow an acceptable dirty perhaps shabby was a better description. Yet today it was even more so. I suppose three years of pristine unadulterated countryside was colouring my view. Here, unlike in West Wales, there was nowhere to hide discarded litter and wanton fly-tipping. In Wales the wooded valleys took care of the odd defunct washing machines and fridges and were lost from view, here people just left them on the street corners and hoped nobody noticed.

I pulled into the car-park and up against the two hundred foot mill chimney and the old folk's bungalow (see Ower Dabbling) stopped the engine and wound down the window. The familiar sound and smell of the crashing of water over the old lock-gates took me instantly back nearly thirty years. Home I thought. Then a smile. You can take the boy out of the North but you can never take the North out of the boy. Sethay!

I think the old lady was glad to see me although the limp in her left leg had grown more pronounced than I remembered. Either that or she was hoping for sympathy. She needn't have bothered. She wouldn't get any. Nurse Rip-it-off, as me and ower kid called her – "It hurts more if yer fiddle wi' it." she would say grumpily as the healing plaster was rent asunder along with half of one's outer layer of skin. Not much sympathy there let me tell yer. As for the old man, one might have thought I had been away for an afternoon, not three years. "Hiya cocky." That was it. Then back to his chrysanthemums, pruning his grape vine and throwing the chickens, the three of them, the left-overs from dinner. The 'prodigal' son returns, went through my mind and the old lady's retort on hearing it -. "Prodigal!" – "Need's a damn sight more than a 'prod'. A bloody good shove - - trouble is we can't find any bridges round here high enough." – Hey-up don't yer just love 'em?

There wouldn't be time for renewing old friendships. A yearning to see what, if anything, might have changed. The town for all its industrial past glories and decline housed a multitude of fascinating wonders some of which went back further than the Doomsday Book's reference to Edward the Confessor's visit in 1046 and his wishes for a short time of rejoicing, although the occasion was somewhat blurred. A hunt for 'game' and if none found a few peasants to roast over a blazing fire. His accompanying Witenagemonts thought he said 'peasants' when in fact the word 'pheasants' had got lost in the translation. One must remember more than four different languages were all straining at the leash for omnipotence in those troubled times. Still the local Thane, known as Gamel the Terrible, was loath to release one of the area's fairest maidens in favour of a few scraggy moorland birds but relented at the point of twenty six pitchforks and numerous cudgels in the hands of the inhabitants from the neighbouring village of Copse.

 A quick visit to the town hall, one of the finest Gothic structures in the whole of the country and a lusting favourite of Adolf Hitler's maniacal dreams, a race up St Chad's ladder, a veritable mountain of ascending stone steps and a panoramic view across the whole town from its loftiest heights alongside the town's oldest church reputed to be from the 11th century. Here, nestling amongst what in the past had been a warren of gravestones, was my point of reference from boy to man - - . No. I did not copulate for the first time on someone's grave. I was brought up better than that. I did however do the 'deed' alongside one such, allowing for a discreet distance (Ower Dawning). One has one's standards you know! Down again past the town's medieval water supply, known as Paker Spout, set neatly alongside what had been the pack-horse route from Yorkshire to the city of Manchester in Anglo-Saxon times and on across the square that held the title 'the widest bridge in the UK' at almost a half a mile wide. Within walking distance the architecture took the mind through every stage of the town's recent history from the Regency periods, the Victorian, the Edwardian interspersed here and there with art-novo, art-deco and modern brutalism and what can only be best described as art-schistose, a rusting Ford Popular on a central raised island of flowers painted in bands of psychedelic vomit. Obviously yet another cunning trickster vying for adulations from the world of art and fart and pay me billions for the products of my troubled disturbed mind. Van Gough's they were not. More like Van-dals if you ask me.

Almost beyond the town's centre, but barely, began the centuries of industry. Firstly alongside the rivers tumbling waters and with the advent of 'steam' almost everywhere one cared to wander. Then neatly ensconced and previously a weavers cottage sat the Co-operative shop. The first one on the planet. Now a museum and lauding that groups amazing success to the business that now trades, under its original people's contract, across large tracts of the world. I had purpose this opportune visit to offer to sell to them my Co-Op jug. (A 'what'?) My Co-Op jug.

"Well it's not rare yer know," said the wizened man from behind his large oak desk. "They was made in their thousands at the time." I nodded sagely. One must always use 'sagely' when negotiating trades. "Ah suppose wi' could g' to a fiver fer it." Five pounds! Go to a fiver! I see. Hm! Not by the way he caressed it almost lovingly amongst his equally wizened palms and gently settled it back upon the desks polished surface. The jug was 1911, a George the Fifth and Mary and, more to the point, was transfer printed for a local store of which there had been only the 'one'. In the manufacture of the jugs, thousands, in the selection of individual stores, perhaps fifty, with the passage of time I suspected no more than two or three actually still existed. The old goat was trying to 'con' me. Did he think I was from out of town - - bless him? He upped the 'anti' to nine quid. I smiled. He frowned. Then I put the jug back in my sling-bag and bade him farewell. Cheeky barsteward.

The town was situated on three sides by the 'Pennine Range' of hills. Not mountains but not hummocks either. The sloping valleys, half a dozen of note, housed everything from derelict Second World War ammunition factories to massive fresh-water lakes and densely packed woodland forests plus glittering cataracts of moorland waters feeding the remains of the glacial river deep in the main valley below. To the young and adventurous a veritable wonderland to be forever explored – but I didn't have time this visit. Not that I hadn't done my exploring many years back and quite often on horseback (Ower Detinue) – in my more barmy years that is – and when our world was fancy free and the truancy officers rarely left the comfort of the town's centre.

It was late when I arrived back at the 'old folks' home. "If ye lookin' fer some tea it's in the dog," smiled the old lady. "Wis eat at five - - - ." "Found what yer were lookin' for then?" If there was one thing I could count on with the old lady it was her almost messianic desire for 'control'. Like a faithful lap-dog it never left her. "No. Not really -." I countered. Let the games begin. "Oh! Was it somethin' special?" "No." I replied. "Not much point in goin' then wus there." she snapped. More of a question than a statement of fact as the sarcasm slipped in. The game had been played since going on fifteen when I realised I had a life, regardless of the fact she had given it to me. Which whenever the subject of children had arisen I made sure to somehow blend into the conversation that 'children are a gift, not a possession – and only for a short time at that'. It never went down well either then or now. "It's getting rougher," said the old man peering sideways through the lounge window and who had waited for a gap in the melee hoping to quell what promised to be another sniping interlude. He was good at filling in gaps. "So's yer bloody skin. Have yer had a shave t'day? Yer beginnin' t' look like one of them there Sally Army's drop-outs," came the swift rebuke. Mother was getting into her stride. The old man curled down the edge of his newspaper and sucked his lips. A sure sign he regretted speaking. "Yes my little swamp-duck," he replied, and slowly sunk back down behind the crumpled newsprint. Hey ho. Nothing much changes then does it!

On my short sojourn I had hoped to tarry awhile alongside areas of my past to take in the 'changes'. Not that my expectations of wonderment would be sated. That would have been too much to ask. More along the lines of curiosity. Had we all 'moved on' so to speak? In the end result it was a melange of mixed emotions. The one up, one down, a house of two rooms one above the other, at William's Place, where I was born during the Second World War (Ower Darkling), and where my first year of a then tenuous existence prevailed, now stood no longer. Nor that of Hope Street, our second abode, a two up two down (yes folks we had gone up in the world) given that with faith house number 13 with its bulging gable end wall and fresh water that came in by way of its cracked slated roof. Both had succumbed to the bulldozers and swinging ball in the 1960's 'clearances' in favour of an endless square block of maisonette flats which, at a glance, impressed me as a modern prison block and from some of the urchins busy scrawling the still pristine brick facades with graffiti, a new generation of ner-do-wells to boot. – That of course was a fleeting impression as such may not have well been the case. At least these homes would have had all the modern comforts when put against the one cold water tap and slab stone sink, the gas mantle lighting, the outside tub toilets, the constant internal dampness and fungal walls and the cockroach ridden interiors of their predecessors. Some things are a 'plus' with progress. Across town some two miles our third abode was still standing, a move that took us from labourers to tradesmen (Ower Dawning). Eleven rooms, if one counted the attic as just the one and a fully enclosed commercial enterprise – a Bakery cum Confectioners cum Cafe and living accommodation. It still had the obligatory outside toilet, but with a proper flush appliance, and no central heating of any kind save for the baking ovens in the lower basements which on a good day percolated throughout the upper rooms if one left all the doors open. It had been akin to moving from a shoebox into a packing case and at just the right time for a seven year old to create havoc. Moving on some three years later, after the mill burnt down and the bustling trade part went out through the window like a fugitive parrot, we kept our trade moniker but reverted back into 'match-box' mode as, yet again, more new premises, again another two miles across town in a different direction, provided three rooms and a shop area. From makers and purveyors of comestibles we are now purveyors of clothes and lingerie for the odd-shaped female which as a ten year old assailed an already confused mind. 'Why would any woman have one tit bigger than the other,' and such like conundrums would harass me for a further few years as I became a number one assistant 'Spirella coseteer fitter' alongside the old lady in order to keep the costs down and not surprisingly my penis up. Yes – I know – beggars belief doesn't it? But that was then and this - - - this is now.

On balance the town was dirtier, rougher, noisier and yet at the same time pleasantly warming, friendly and comfortingly familiar. That was ower old town.

The later years and in between times, that was from divesting myself of a number of businesses as previous readers will have gleaned and before saying goodbye to the Owd Town, we tarried in a new purpose built town-house on the edge of the moor but yet still in sight of the dilapidated monstrous, numerous cotton mills that blanketed the valley from end to end. It would be difficult to say the air was much cleaner there but it was good to get the freshness of them as they rolled down the steepness of the slopes before mingling with their carbon layered pathfinders in the cluttered streets a couple of hundred feet below.

I suppose now is a good time to explain why a born and bred Northern lad might want to leave his ancient roots – but can people handle the truth? "Tha's bloody barmy. Wha'd yer want t' do that fer? It's no greener tha' knows". But in truth I am witness that it is. Or at least the greenery is – by a mile if not lots more. But in truth my twenty years of self-employment amongst the rat-race of business and its grotesque, two-faced machinations on the one hand and the economics of a 'landed' change on the other drove me in the only logical direction forward. Away. Far away. To a place where the nearest neighbour would have to put himself out by hiking miles if he wished to borrow a half-flagon of my finest home-made mead. The high peaks of north-west Scotland fitted the bill, but I relented on the damage it would possibly rent upon my fair Anglo-Saxon complexion (not to mention my nether regions) and plunged instead for the smoother hills and valleys of Wild West Wales.

Our arrival, as aforementioned, caused little stirring amongst the indigenous population of the valley. My wife Valerie, she who must at least be listened to, and my flaxen blonde six years old daughter Cara, she who only need bat an eyelid to secure forgiveness, both in accompaniment. Together with our horses, dogs, cats and quickly added to goats, chickens, ducks, geese and a hamster called Fred all about to savour the delights of this old 'new world'. Dreams people. Dreams.

Let me tell you about dreams. Unless you are in reality a genuine realist. Don't even dream them. I suppose at one time, especially In my youth I must have been there, considering I view myself as 'normal'. Yes I know that wasn't in my parent's estimation. But – hey – parents, who listens to those! Silly old farts for the most part, not to mention antiquated and most certainly 'not with it'. Who wouldn't appreciate 'Little Richard' and 'Screaming Lord Sutch' – what do they know? You can't take people seriously who denigrate such geniuses.

Not surprisingly I wasn't the only one around who dabbled in dreams. It seems I had landed fair and square in 'Dreamland' itself.

'Never-Never Land'.

"Is it supposed to look like that -?" I remember a distinct long silence before a very strained reply.

"Like what - - ?"

"Like that – like the side of a rusty three penny bit -?"

The shimmering slopes of my foreman carpenters white sideburns, known as Johnnie Greybeard, stood out distinctly from the sides of his face. His eyes, normally pig-slatted, seemed to sink even deeper into their narrow holes. The conversation halted at that precise point. Nothing more was said - until the following morning.

"Hey-up Boss. Some lousy bastard's nicked the handles off the coach doors." – "What?" – – Barrackroom began again. "I said – some lousy - ." "Yes, yes. I heard what you said."

It was true. The railway carriage, newly under construction, was indeed minus its door handles. Also, as it happened minus its carpenter and his tool boxes.

This was a serious discussion for the members of the Railway Society. One absent carpenter. They couldn't decide what to do so they shuffled it sideways to the 'Coach and Wagons Committee' who also determined they didn't know what to do either.

"It's must be matter for the Board of Directors," said the Chairman of the CWC.

The Board of Directors were not due a meeting until the first of the month, some three weeks away. So it was decided to call a 'SGM' immediately. The 'SGM' was called for the next day. Totally against the rules of the Constitution, but this was urgent, "We can't deal with this. It's really down to the 'Project Steering Committee," said the Chairman glancing about himself. "Yes Mr Chairman. But aren't we, some of us, the Project Steering Committee?" asked a confused but slightly more momentarily alert director The Chairman's greying eyes seemed to be following his greying despair as he groaned, "Duw. Duw.No,no. There are two missing from the Society. We can't convene a PSC without notification to the CWC and the Society. All hell would break loose bach." And so the CWC/ Society were notified – the very next day.

I related all this to give you, dear reader, a small inkling of just how some of our heritage railway organisations are cobbled together. Organisation they may well be termed, organised – they are most certainly not and those that show some semblance of a unified construct are simply good at camouflaging their own self-destructive processes. The term 'a dog's dinner' is without doubt a compliment.

And it all comes in the first place from 'dreams'. Dreams, dreams, dreams, dreams, dreams, dreams –.

Why Johnnie Greybeard, the carpenter, was in charge of track-laying came about because of his expertise at previous NG (narrow gauge) railways he had been involved with. Had he made plain he was no longer welcome at most of them everything may well have been different. Alas, he hadn't. The reference from a director of the railway and chairman of the PSC to 'the sides of a rusty three penny bit' was the last straw. The man just couldn't take any more. He could however take his carriage/coach door handles, his tools and himself off the 'project' and go home, as it happened, on full pay for the next three months, leaving yours truly with thirty percent less responsible management and seventeen disreputable labourers grinning like Cheshire cats.

"We desperately need a rail-bender." said Mr Whiskers or as he had previously quipped a few weeks earlier, some diminutive strong-necked Welsh miners. And so a rail-bender was acquired along with a robust security-safe in which to keep it. Gold bullion didn't come cheaper.

Mid-way through the term of the 'contract' at a time when the 'lads' had become accustomed to the concept of 'work' – some of whom had actually begun to enjoy it – the PSC lost its chairman. He hadn't died. He had simply disappeared one afternoon. One minute he was with the steering group mulling over safety rails in the gorge, the next – poof – gone. Naturally the committee searched the hillside and the bottom of the gorge for battered remains. But found none. "Duw, duw. There's a mystery. Bit of a problem that. He was down for judging the 'Finest Marrow' at the Llangeler village show this week-end. Tch. Bit of a blow that isn't it?"

It did however solve the problem of my foreman carpenter and the carriage door-handles who returned himself and the missing items refusing as he did so to lay not an inch more track and 'you know what you can do with your rail-bender'. Bit of a relief all around if you ask me.

Such was a constant problem with the 'volunteer' side of the equation. Here one minute, gone the next, which was quite often when the particular volunteer had been in the middle of a specific task vital to the continuance of the 'projects'. Woe betide he or she who desired for the 'plan' to succeed. Such was never on the cards. "Finished! No,no. Duw, duw boyo. Finished! You're in Wales. You can't finish things. That will never do. Do that and you will have nothing to do tomorrow -?"

And so one battled on with the finished contract date looming ever closer and closer and winter again fast approaching.

"The appropriation, without authorisation, of namely one new tyre for his own vehicle!" Such was the charge. A hush fell around the confines of the room. The clink of beer glasses from outside in the bar took over the proceedings. Previously the board of directors had met, considered the complaint from one of its own and determined that the overseeing authority, in this case the local county council, would have to handle the matter forthwith. And so it came to pass. Barrackroom suggested I wear a chain, the kind they sell in garden centres for delineating lawn areas and a cistern ball – all painted black and attach them to my ankle. "If yer drag yer foot as you enter. It'll make it all the more lifelike," he grinned.

At this juncture it is necessary to explain that for life to exist and continue apace human beings must have enemies or as ower old lady once said –" If the buggers can't find sumat t' fight each other about, especially the Irish, then they'll scrap over how many harp strings there are on the label of a Guinness bottle." Likewise all societies and most particular volunteer organisations, who it would seem spend more time plotting against each other than sleeping. I was aware there were those that didn't like me. But staggered at the lengths some would go to malign and destroy no matter how beneficial or useful I might have been towards the 'projects' purposes. Homo homini et lupus est. Or words to that effect. But given only Eleanor, she of the patterned flowered frock, would have understood them I declined, at that juncture, to place them on offer.

The 'charge' was 'misappropriation of project funds'. But to understand how such may have arisen one needs to know exactly 'how' the project actually worked – if one could use such a euphemism. MSC or Manpower Services Commission was a government sponsored stop-gap arrangement to reduce the unemployment figures which at that time stood at plus three million. Put the idle and the unfortunates to work, pay them a bog-standard wage and make everyone feel good. It didn't – but who cares. The individual projects were overseen by the local councils who had the final word on any and all decisions. Therefore, misappropriation of funds came under their remit. The council could, if it wished, close down any project at a moments notice in the event of 'trouble at mill' regardless of the worth of the project or the trauma from such actions that would have inevitably followed. Abject fear reigned within those organisations – such as the Railway – so much so should such as this come to pass that the vast majority of misdemeanours very rarely got beyond the gates of the railway. This time, on this day of infamy, it appeared one of the board of directors couldn't have cared less and really did have it 'in for me'. It was to be hoped the day went well for if not the whole 'dream' could come crashing down and the 'puffer-nutter's nirvana disappear faster than a rabid rat up a rusty drainpipe.

'Not guilty' as charged. 'Guilty of misuse of projects stationary'. Fined – one days pay. Thus allowing the 'dream train' to trundle on. Everyone was happy, apart from my accuser, who couldn't be named. It came to pass I must have had some friends in amongst the powers that be for within a month my accuser was dismissed from the board of directors and unceremoniously bundled overboard without a good-service handshake. - - and so the band played on.

It was time to take stock. The month of November appeared on the calendar – we had one of those, albeit in Welsh, which apart from the numbers no-one could understand – and barely a fortnight from the end of 'Scheme One'. 'Scheme Two' had already been secured as Eleanor, with her 'Masters Degree', was at no pains to triumph across the valley. The problem was Scheme One wasn't finished. Imagine the situation. Everyone employed upon the first scheme was to be made redundant, including yours truly. A new 'team' and new 'management' was to be found and a new work-programme to be instituted. Continuity wasn't included in the new round of financing and any joined-up thinking succinctly and adroitly outlawed.

"Well now bach. You see. If you was a member of the society we could offer you up as an overseer you see. No pay. Voluntary. A sort of keeper of the railways interests isn' it." In other words, come and work seven days a week, be responsible for the project and answer to the board of directors – and starve at the same time! Sounded eminently sensible to me.

I blame the Welsh air. Laced with ganja. Or perhaps the cawl soup and larva-bread. Whatever, it definitely worked. With millions still unemployed, volunteer work was classed as semi-employment to which the remaining 'semi' the State turned a blind eye. At forty years old I was quite ready, after the previous twenty-five years amongst the lunatics, to play my own game and await results. I was also a father again. This time a boy. I had tried to persuade 'she who must at least be listened to' that dogs were a better idea. We now had six, dogs that is. But it hadn't worked. So much for best laid plans and enter a tiny version of myself -. Ooops!

'It is 1985 in a Welsh valley and 'she who must at least be listened to' demands progeny, animals we have 'everywhere', a lifetime of trouble – well – that's another story. Hail a son, Sean. And the story continues.

'Christmas Comes Early'

"You steady it. I'll hit it." 'Thwack'. The dresser base shuddered as the flannel sized chain-mail crashed against its surface. We peered closely at it together.

"Hmmmm -." I could tell by the tone from Lionel Bravehearts throat he wasn't entirely satisfied.

"Hit it again – but a bit harder." I ventured.

"Hmmm. I think it needs some more patination. Force it deeper otherwise when you come to the 'scorching' it may leave some new wood showing – - can't have that."

We were constructing another original Tudor style dog-kennel Welsh dresser from a design I remembered seeing in Haddon Hall some years back, with an open backed rack and wrought iron nail hooks. Elizabethan of the first order - in the day of Elizabeth of the second order. At a pinch it could fetch upwards of four hundred pounds at a local auction and sell in London for fourteen hundred. A nice day out if one was prepared to speculate. – Needs must when the devil drives.

As the 'unpaid' project overseer of the railways MSC Scheme Two for five days a week, the remainder, plus one or two late nights, helped provide the wherewithal to survive. The 'good-life' of the countryside was very intermittent with its 'good' but frequently made up for its bounty by providing the weather and the wildlife with ample means to destroy it. Slugs ate the lettuce, butterflies ate the cabbages, rabbits ate the carrots, the fox ate the chickens and the goats ate everything in sight, including the washing off the line, if they escaped. Which they had a knack at doing the minute one's back was turned. As for the horses they just ate and ate and ate and ate. The muck-midden looked like a London tower-block. Tenzing Norgay could have trained his Himalayan Sherpa's on it with relative safety given previously well informed directions.

The Welsh dresser looked resplendent in its deep dark oak staining and two coats of Fiddes magical wax furniture polish. "Could do half a grand in Cardiff." Lionel stood back for a better angle of viewing. "We'll take it with us next hospital appointment. Kill two birds with one stone." "Hmm -." - - I stood back. Perhaps with a new rubber in my catapult such might have been possible but to my mind the cornice was still too 'only yesterday' for my liking although we had split it in three places and fudged it together again to give it that battered look.

 Lionel was a haemophiliac, an ancient disease (reputedly from royal stock) which meant he bled easily and continuously both internally and externally from even the slightest cut or abrasion and which was why he had chosen a profession as a master carpenter. Chisels, hammers, saws and drills - -what can go wrong?

"I have Christmas disease," he said. "Not your ordinary haemophilia. Mines special. Costs twice as much as your common-o-garden stuff. Fifteen grand a throw. We are 'the crème de la crème' of the awkward brigade. Specials – the kid glove treatments." As I was to discover the naming came from the first patient to be discovered with this particular strain of the disease – one James Christmas and not, as one might have thought, from the name of the medical genius who separated and diagnosed it from all the rest. Strange world -! Once every three months we made the round trip of three hundred miles to replenish his 'stocks' of 'factor nine' (the injections required to stop the bleeds) whether or not they had been used. A total of sixty thousand pounds per annum in a bid to keep himself alive. Plus and not to mention (so I will) the added costs of the disabled mobility benefits etc, etc, etc, which averaged another forty thousand pounds per annum. He was a nice guy. Which was just as well as otherwise and under different circumstances and given my propensity to often be blunt I may well have baulked at his very existence on the planet. In conclusion and given all this country's other ills we should all thank some of our far-seeing forefathers, in particular one Aneurin Bevan for its inception and one Winston Churchill, who rescued it from the hands of some founder detractors, for their empathy and sense of fair-play, on the existence of the National Health Service and our Welfare State. We live in a country well-blessed by any other measure of present day humanity.

We christened Christmas with a visit to the Christmas Ward in the country's capital hospital and crowned out the week at the local auction house by snatching six hundred and twenty five pounds for the 'new' antique dresser. A very good start towards the New Year.

Scheme Two of 'mission impossible railway' had been trimmed. A compliment of nineteen budding 'workers' and one manager and a reduction in available funds to ninety thousand pounds with which to work the next miracle. Two miles of nature trail with accompanying fences. One woodland amphitheatre to seat three hundred persons. One log-bog dividable by two to seat four persons. One carriage shed to house four locomotives and two carriages and one settling tank with five hundred yards of drainage thereto. In addition, but not on the contract, one ticket office, one cafe, one water tower – work to be carried out by the volunteers and – search parties to ascertain the whereabouts of hitherto mentioned but quite often invisible- volunteers.

With a compliment of one hundred and fifty railway society members it was expected that around fifteen percent would be fit and able to attend and further the projects ambitions. I could usually count upon five or six which even with my detestation of maths and anything remotely to do with schooling didn't reach such lofty heights as those far-flung and intangible 'great expectations'. The often used phrase of 'one willing volunteer is worth more than ten pressed men' may have been good enough for the Great Wall of China but totally useless when used in the Welsh context. "For nothing is it?" the first question when trying to raise volunteers. –A brief pause followed with

-. "Duw, duw. Does you do a lot of that in England then bach?"

But to be truthful as regards the 'project', without the dreams and actions from many of Welsh extraction, buoyed on by even many more of English lineage, I would not now be standing at the bottom of the steep wooded slope trying to imagine, with scepticism, row upon row of terraced wooden seating and thinking to myself – why did I ever dream of leaving my Northern home-? Yet more to the point. Which toss-pot mentioned 'railway'? Although to be honest a 'woodland amphitheatre' was my idea and nothing at all to do with the 'puffer-nutter fraternity'. It was on the tourist entertainment part of the scheme and a part of the natural escapism into 'things to do' for the visitor who had never seen a real woodland or even had the opportunity to walk through one. Here was an example of something untouched for centuries about to be laid open by machete wielding, chainsaw and axe bearing ganja growers. And not too delicately either.

"Fuck."

"No Bellend. We don't have time for that and – it's not on the programme for today's work schedule." I waved the clip-board to accentuate the point. "Nowhere on here does it list those. It does list ballast-truck which whose wheels, if you remember, you forgot to chock last night and which is now lying upside down at the bottom of the gorge minus the truck part – and its load of ballast." Bellend held up the bloodied stump of the forefinger of his left hand. "I've chopped mi' bleedin' finger orf." I allowed sufficient a pause before -. "No. That's incorrect lad. You have chopped the end off your finger which is bleeding." I replied. "And, not to put too fine a point on it, which you could have done had you cut it at more of an angle, you're a fucking disaster area all on your own." Bellend, real name Bradley, but a name he was very well suited to, took a few moments to decipher the words. "Well, you could fire me," came an eventual retort. "No I can't. It's not allowed." I bellowed in exasperation. "Get back to the yard and have one of the lads take you to the doctors or better still the hospital -." I gestured towards the small lump amongst the pool of blood lying atop a tangle of the brambles. " – and take the rest of you along as well. Your presence as a whole is bad enough without you leaving bits of you all over the place." - - - Pillock- (a thought, not a voiced statement).

The track-bed leading off along the valley ran downhill to the nearest town some four miles distant. Any rolling-stock left on-line unattended, even chocked and braked, could end up in the deep gorge just over a mile down, for not only did we have our own 'vandals' on the site but the local village had its fair share of miscreants always willing to assist in mayhem, at the drop of a Welsh leek, to brighten their days.

"Do you think you could have a few words with your son?" I asked, almost as if passing. Policy Jones one of our rare volunteers and known as such because he was the local Insurance Broker, stopped chipping away at the rust caking the iron rungs of an old water-tower scaling ladder and removed his goggles. "Er - - -. Which few words would you suggest bach?" Typically Welsh. Answer a question with a question. "Well – words like. 'Stop being a bloody nuisance', for starters. You could add 'The fence railings are not for kicking off' and 'the small children's play-area is for small children not testosterone brain-mangled teenagers'." Policy Jones went into depression mode. The Welsh are a good people but prone to extremes. They are either 'up' or 'down'. There doesn't seem to be space for any in-between. Unlike we English who can always be on any rung of the emotion ladder from top to bottom depending upon the time of day and the weather. I tarried a moment. I could see movement behind the eyes. "Righto bach." He turned and replaced the goggles. Well that had been easier than I had first thought. Although I doubted it would do any good. "Right. Fine." I muttered - - -. Next - - - . Give me strength.

It's painful but necessary to be acquainted with the hierarchy and incomprehensible workings of many of the Heritage Railway companies. Why? Because no-one of sound mind and body would purposely set out to produce such a supposed 'working body'. Not consciously that is.

It comprised of a Limited Liability company attached loosely to which a 'society' and the various offshoot consortiums intertwined themselves at various points each with various constitutions and standing orders by which they could toss spanners into the whole mass of machinery thus bringing the whole workings to a shuddering halt at all or any critical point. In other words producing 'a tail wagging a dog'. Having come from the world of private enterprise I struggled for many months to come to terms with what I considered to be chaos and disorder. Try as I may I was never successful at understanding this weird form of so called 'democracy' and to this day it still amazes me how so many of them continue to survive. I'm told that the bigger the organisation, member wise, the more successful they become, as those in charge can instil an absolute form of discipline whereby individual members 'fight' for inclusion. But with a membership of less than a local sewing circle each member became an indispensable God-like creature and thus a set battle-piece for constant warfare for position and influence ensues. It is into this, dear friend's I have descended. Almost sacrificially.

At this point the 'railway' has a ten year history, not the original 'broad gauge' of Brunel's time, but that of its saviours the 'Whitland & Llanboidy Angels of Steam Brigade' led by a well respected local doctor of good repute. 'Save our Railway' had become the order of the day- - - so try and save it they did. Another doctor of less than good repute, a Doctor Beeching and government hatchet man, had designs otherwise. Of the one hundred miles of rural lines being 'axed', as in done away with in this location, the Angels of Steam managed to save just twelve and it was towards this went tens of thousands of voluntary man-hours of verbal struggle and boisterous strife.

A compressed version of events which included the purchase of the track-beds, bridges, crossings and platforms but which excluded any rail, buildings, gateways, signage or services was then followed by a Bill to Parliament for permission to adapt the land for a Narrow-Gauge railway and the raising of the large sums of monies to complete the process which took up most of the intervening years. Waiting for no man, and experiencing a sense of relief, nature had woven her magic spell obliterating the industrial passage of man's endeavours with her usual distain of 'cop for that omnipotent's' and a further, 'screw with me at your peril', challenge, whereupon entered yours truly with his trusty new bush saw, machete and shiny black-japanned mattock. - - What did I think I was doing!

We went off and found a 'cafe'. It stood on a large concrete base in a village near Whitland, a village west of Swansea, and had seen better days. For fifty years it had served as a 'Boy Scouts hut' but had outlived its occupants 'dibbing and dobbing' and two and three-fingered salutes and was now destined to serve a further fifty years, after a complete make-over, sheltering members and visitors alike astride the ancient copings of the now recently resurrected railway yard's cattle stand. Given a new coat of GWR (Great Western Railway) paintwork, it turned out, looking the part, alongside the new pristine toilet-block and given the name 'Cafe' in large white letters so as not to confuse the two.

"Are you sure that is really necessary?" I asked. Mr Whiskers looked at me askance. "But of course. Absolutely imperrrrative. Duw, duw. They's English visitors. Tourists. Can't have them wandering about holding it in bach. They comes on holidays and leaves half their brains at home -." he tapped at his woollen bobble hat -. "Stopped working. Half asleep. Got to give them directions properly boyo." One doesn't argue with a Welsh minor/miner who has a hankering for half size steam locomotives and a beard ideally suited for a Father Christmas look-alike come the Santa Specials - - if the project ever gets that far, and so to make everything acceptable towards half-brain dead visitors Mr Whiskers delivered up a pine board sign with the words 'Toilet', inscribed thereon -. "Can't have them wandering into the loos looking for a cup of tea now can we." he chortled.

Christmas approached. Also the culmination of 'Scheme Two'. One final push and we would have a viable 'Tourist N.G. Railway' attraction. But the lady was not for turning. Eleanor that is.

"There's some money left." A hush descended across the room. Complete silence reigned for a full five seconds. This was a statement rarely heard in these forgotten valleys. "Left!" croaked the Chairman. "Er – left where?" Eleanor shuffled her stack of papers.

"Apparently the County Council need to spend around a quarter of a million pounds before the end of March. They were wondering did we want any of it?" The eleven company directors, apparently there were nineteen in total but a full compliment didn't fit into the 'snug' room of the local public house comfortably and hence the numbers worked on a rota system, went into a catatonic trance. This was a situation they had never come across before. Normally they spent most of their time battling against the County Council to avoid paying the local taxes. Being offered council money was an entirely insurmountable problem. It was eventually left to Eleanor, the company secretary, she of the flowered patterned frocks, to make of it what she could. Hence we arrived at - - - 'Scheme Three'.

'Boy Scout hut 'Cafe' and New Toilet Block'.

Mr & Mrs Goodlife.

"The chickens have gone daft again." She, who must at least be listened to, removed the night's production of crap splattered eggs from her apron to the washing up bowl. "It's all that heavy rock music they've been listening to all night. – Procol Harem or whatever it is." One of the neighbours on the opposite side of the valley had taken to all night sessions of an endless cacophony of mind-numbing beat music which sallied forth willy-nilly for miles around on its way to the Irish Sea. One didn't question the underlying causes. This was Welsh Wales where such dalliances were often commonplace. "T'is the fresh air bach. Fuddles the clockworks." said Mr Whiskers. "They's got to get acclimatised. Takes a while. No good rrrremonstrating. They can be violent – isn' it." As this was the second time with the chickens in three days I wandered off to check. To ignore the wife's pointed statement could have lasting consequences for the rest of the day.

Sure enough the chickens had gone daft. A number had taken to throwing themselves sideways every other hesitant step whilst some were just lying upside down eyeballing the sky as if waiting for some curious unsuspecting hawk to descend for an easy meal. As I approached, the rooster, the one that used to attack everything within twenty yards, rolled out from beneath the caravan. It belly-flopped at my feet wobbling its spurs in frustrated annoyance that it couldn't as usual, raise itself towards my exposed throat. This was a conundrum. In the old days, back home, we set down traps for them, conundrums that is. We never caught any but it wasn't from the want of trying. A cigarette was called for. I knelt before the prostrated cockerel, removed a cigarette from its packet and raised my lighter to ignite it. It was then I noticed a strange odour. It seemed to be almost at ground level. A sort of cold almost nutty smell. Whatever it was it had no business being in my back garden. Something clicked. The hens hadn't gone beat-crazy. They had been gassed. The only possibility of 'gas' in this part of Wales came in bottles or long standing septic tanks. The temperature of the previous two nights before had been well below zero. The chickens used the underside of the caravan for dust-bathing, which was also where the gas bottles stood that fed the caravan's utilities. It was fortuitous I hadn't lit my cigarette. Or it's doubtful I would be writing this 'good-life' scenario today. A quick check showed a collar of icing around one of the main connectors and an almost red level on the pressure gauges. Mystery solved - - and catastrophe averted. Just another day in the countryside. There would be 'eggs' today and eggs tomorrow and the cockerel would have learned, at long last, some respect for my magical subduing powers.

In the modern age being closeted in some remote rarely trodden area doesn't mean the world passes you by. You can always guarantee some well meaning artefact or person will assail you with the madness that still prevails in the land of the homo-sapiens. We are at war with Argentina or the Americans. Greenham Common and the tree-huggers have surrounded an American base to stop nuclear war with their banjos, bangles and beads and lot's of sitting down and wailing. Meanwhile a new fangled technology called the Internet has arrived and quartz watches and someone has found Hitler's Diaries. If they had asked I could have told them he never wrote any. Not even a poem or the odd sea-shanty They turned out forgeries - - doh! Lionel, he of the Braveheart, suggested a trip to the capitol – no, not London. Cardiff. A seminar of vital importance. There was a new virus on the block. A potential killer. HTLV 3 (AIDS) and blood products could potentially carry it. It cannot really be said I have a puncheon for the intricacies of medical science but something told me it wouldn't be a waste of a day out and a good excuse to relax for a little while from the madness of 'railway'. As it transpired that day's information would come to haunt the medical world as whose consequences mirrored and surpassed that of the Thalidomide scandal of a previous decade. The Scourge of Lyon, Klaus Barbie, the Nazi butcher had been extradited from Bolivia where he had hidden away from Mossad, the Israeli Intelligence Services, and the world's Nazi hunters, thus aided and abetted by the intelligence services of the U.S.A, for almost forty years. The French people didn't guillotine him and he died in prison some eight years on. Not what some would call 'justice'. But then wars never produce such luxuries.

'Hurrah'. We beat the Argies (Argentineans) and killed a few hundred innocents into the bargain. The Union flag flies again over a barren group of islands in the South Atlantic of which most Britons have never heard of and couldn't locate even if you gave them an Atlas. On the shoulders of victory Maggie Thatcher now rides triumphantly into a second term of office in Downing Street as the Americans triumphantly invade one of our Caribbean islands without telling us or at least warning us first. Grenada -? Where's that? And why?

The first Space Shuttle was launched and the building of an International Space Station began. With ground-breaking satellites came the first G.P.S. (Ground positioning). "Load er crap." exclaimed Curly, "Yow only need the sun and a wrist watch to tell yow where's yow are." Curly was from Birmingham. We called him Curly after the Crow Scout and sole survivor of Custer's Last Stand on the Little Big Horn and not because of his straight black hair, but because he was an excellent 'tracker' of all 'things' lost (including recalcitrant workers) or borrowed or stolen.

The lady tree-huggers from Greenham Common's A.A.F Base needn't have worried as a world saviour was in our midst's, one Major Stanislav Petrov who managed single-handedly to avert a Third World War by refusing to press the Soviet Union's nuclear button. A Nuclear Alarm depicting a nuclear attack went off by mistake. The Major, adroitly knowledgeable with Russian technology, refused to believe the clamour of bells and flashing lights and switched everything off at the mains – whereupon the screens went blank. They were also blank when he switched them back on again – thankfully. I think secretly he was quietly shipped to Siberia for a well-deserved long winter holiday.

Meanwhile, back on the ranch, my own pocket-sized version, the villagers were revolting. Something was decimating their lovingly attended gardens, ripping asunder flower-beds and privet hedges alike. Clues in the form of hoof prints and goat droppings led the pitchfork brigade to my door demanding retribution and compensation. "Your goats boyo. Trampling and chomping they is. My buddleia's buggerrred. To the roots. Gone! Puff! Five years it was. Beau-tiful. Beau-tiful. Buggerrred it is now. Completely buggerrred." I listened attentively, as one must, to the list of complaints. I couldn't see how my goats could have possibly scaled the garden fences tethered as they were during the day by rope and rubber tyres allowing only for small movements in a circular fashion. At night they were housed in their own barred and padlocked wooden barn structure. It just wasn't possible. It was another conundrum – blasted things. The villagers retreated, grudgingly, following a worthwhile promise I would look into the matter. At length, as the destruction clandestinely continued, I put Curly on it. A mere twenty-four hours elapsed before the 'railway's tracker' presented his conclusions.

"Yows got Nubians," he declared. "Good Lord. Have we?" That came as a bit of a shock. "Is it contagious?" Curly mulled it over. You could see he hadn't considered that particular aspect. Then at length.

"Only if yow let's them shag each other," he replied. I relaxed. The 'Billy' wasn't allowed access. "Bright little bastards Nubians. Not yows ordinary Welsh types. Crafty. Yow's got t' watch them." - - "Yow come with me." Curly led us to the side of the wooden barn. "Yow watch." With the tips of two fingers he pressed upon the wooden boarding. The boards pivoted inwards revealing a hole the size of a large dog-flap at ground level through which a small horned head eventually appeared. Curly stuck his boot on it. "Crafty little buggers," he said. "Yow needs a hammer and some nails. Not for the goats. Yower shed." I left Curly on guard whilst I went in search of the appropriate items and wondered by what avenue of compensation might the pitchfork brigade be assuaged? Goats milk perhaps? Hmmm! Perhaps, given in the round, that really would be a little too cheeky all things considered.

"Where I came from you never picked it up if you didn't know what it was or understand it." Mr Thomas the Headmaster of the primary school looked at me over the top of his bi-focals, as if two pair of optical lenses wasn't enough. "If you did there was the off-chance it might go 'boom' and blow yer bloody head off." I replied. His apparent knowledge of children and their abilities to 'pick things up', by which I assumed he meant everything from lolly-sticks to diphtheria, but in this case the Welsh language, left me with a feeling of unease. The school was of the Victorian era in build, similar to the one I was incarcerated in my infancy, but with a thoroughly modernised interior. Someone here obviously thought learning by gas-light didn't promote a well-rounded product. It was supposed to be bi-lingual, Welsh and English, but leaned heavily towards its indigenous roots."If they don't instantly understand they copy what the others are doing. Children are very adaptable." he replied. Hmm! Copy. I remember that. Do that at my school and get thrashed to within an inch of one's life. I shuddered and brushed it aside. As for adapting. You could get expelled for that in my day. "Well she did adapt. She smacked him on the nose for using foul language." "Duw.duw. No, no. Not at all. He was speaking in Welsh. T'wasn't rrrude. T'was quite clean so the boy says." And therein lay the nub of the problem. It was all lost to the ether in the translation and the potential lies. I mulled it over for a second or two as it wasn't worth much more. "Well there we are then. Was the lad upset?" Mr Thomas allowed himself a similar brief moment before "Well he wasn't verrry happy. Nearly broke his nose she did. Bright red it is." It was the only time I had deigned to enter the school, or for that matter any school at all since I was fifteen, having had an aversion towards them since that stressed out youthful time. Today it would be called P.T.S.D or Post traumatic stress disorder but today she, who at least must be listened to, had a previous engagement elsewhere which left me with no alternative but to take the plunge. "Is he pressing charges?" I thought it expedient to go for the jugular. I could feel my nerves beginning to give way as the walls seemed to be growing slowly inwards.

"No,no,no, nooo. We doesn't do 'charges'. It's the aggrrrression you see. Very agrresive she was. Something about rrripping his bits and pieces off. - - Very alarrrming." That sounded familiar. From my mothers side. Obviously a chip off that old block. I smiled. "She doesn't mean it. She growls a lot. Just to keep things in order. She will have forgotten it in a couple of days." Mr Thomas wasn't convinced. I could tell by the way he kept glancing sideways at me and how his cheek kept twitching. I wondered how long it would take for him to give up this particular episode and move on. I wasn't about to get any further involved with how the man ran his school, always and providing my children came home at the end of the day in one piece. A bright red nose wouldn't have fazed me.

It was a Saturday. I remember that quite distinctly. It should have been a relaxing day as the 'railway gang' only worked a five-day week. Monday to Friday. Saturday was my day and the day before the 'railway volunteers' trickled in looking for as little to do as possible – apart from going to the pub – and another excuse not to go to 'chapel', when the telephone rang. It was Richard of Whitland. My reverie slumped - slightly. Richard rarely rang for a chat. More a seminar which could last an hour or two. God knows what the size his telephone bill was. Not to put too fine a point on it but could I meet a man from CADEW – a qaungo – a quasi autonomous non-governmental organisation – at the castle in the town half an hour ago. It had slipped his mind. Richard was what is euphemistically known as a 'Puffer Nutter'. Not of the train-spotting anorak brigade, more of the hands-on and inside and all over it brigade. Richard could tell you from a pile of rust, the date, the origin, the history and the provenance of something that looked like it had been discarded from the back of a rag and bone man's cart and describe its use in the terms of an art specialist oozing over the finer points of the Mona Lisa. Yes folks. He was a bloody bore. But ever such a kind and nice chap.

I shouldn't have said 'yes' – but I did.

The castle (as seen below) had a rugged rural beauty all of its own. Obviously because no-one else would have wanted it. From where I hail it would have been considered as a pile of dilapidated old stones in want of removal and but for the concrete capping, to keep the structure together, would most certainly have disappeared for hardcore under some renovation of granolithic back-yard coverings.

"Duw, duw. No. Not indeed." came the retort in reply to my observation to –"I'm amazed it hasn't been lifted for road-fill." "It is prrrotected you see. Historrical it is. Been here for a long time it has. Centurries."

The man from CADW had agreed to visit the ancient monument following a query from the railway's Board of Directors as to the viability of a station platform and pathways on the castle grounds. At this point I won't attempt to outline the background of the 'plans' for expansion as the railway wasn't as yet 'a railway', something I thought I should mention just in passing. "Visions boyo. Visions. Got to have them. Without visions there will be no realities. Prrrogress requires visions." I didn't comment further. To explain that I was working for a cohort of excessive dreamers who had yet to arrive and buy a ticket for 'visions' seemed superfluous to say the least. The man produced a field-tape and for the next hour I stood at various points around the stone ruin as he took a series of measurements. Finally it came on to rain, a rapid squall which signalled an abrupt end to the proceedings. "Someone will contact you bach, - eventually," he said scurrying away up and down and down and up the ancient pathway of the fortifications towards the distant car-park. I stood, dripping, as I watched him go, remembering my utter distaste of cold water, especially down the back of my neck. I had been here in Wales long enough to know that whatever the weather when one sets out one should always pack a sou-wester and wellington boots – or suffer the consequences.

'Never On A Sunday'.

"And we've not yet been to the pub!" Mr Whiskers raised a hand to his woollen hat and swivelled the bobble, his eyes not leaving the bend in the cab's stanchion and the buckled footplate beneath. Five minutes previously, when all had been right with the world and I was deep in conversation with Johnnie Greybeard and Mr Whiskers on the next addition towards the completion of the project when the gable wall of the concrete garage behind which we were standing suddenly surged towards us. I wasn't aware old men of that age could move quite so fast. "Shit -," came a strangled cry from somewhere amongst the furling dust cloud. I was quite taken aback. I couldn't remember hearing Mr Whiskers use a profanity in all the few years I had known him. As for Johnnie Greybeard I didn't think he knew any. We gathered on the edge of the cement cloud and peered towards its innards. There was a distinctive bout of coughing as slowly from within there appeared a human form grey from head to toe with arms flailing as if fending off a swarm of angry bees. It was Leith from Neath. A volunteer engine driver – soon to become 'as was'.

"I only left it for a couple of seconds." he gasped turning back towards the steam locomotive which was protruding from the rubble issuing a high pressure jet of steam – obviously in annoyance – from one of its broken injector pipes. "Would that be your brain bach?" muttered Mr Whiskers wishing to voice it louder but well aware of the lack of any volunteers however inept. Leith from Neath slowly surveyed the wreckage. "I'm sure I put the brake on – I'm positive. Positive it is -." Mr Whiskers tugged at his bobble. "Was that before you neutralised the rrregulator – or after - bach?" The question seemed to stump the concrete grey countenance of the Neath volunteer as he struggled trying to decide which answer he should pick. Although any qualified steam locomotive driver would have scowled in distain at such an affront to his knowledge.

We never did get an answer. Half an hour later Leith from Neath was missed when it was his turn to buy the next round as the volunteer gang for the day repaired to the pub to discuss concrete panels and where to get replacements. Johnnie Greybeard had the answer. Tongued and grooved weather boarding and copious amounts of mastic- well he was after all a carpenter and a wall is a wall is a wall when all's said and done. Even if it does house a very expensive, narrow-gauge, slate-quarry, steam locomotive.

Scheme Three and again I was seconded as Project Manager – unpaid. With interest rates in double figures, inflation on the rampage and three million still unemployed the scheme applications were over-subscribed, until the second day of the project when the applicants had discovered what it was they were being asked to do. "Where is everybody?" Daft question. By midday we reached a compliment of ten unwilling participants and by the following morning, after discovering they would all be losing their unemployment benefits, everybody returned to the site. Some actually arriving on time.

For the woodland amphitheatre- stone barbeques, picnic areas, drainage channelling, bat boxes and woodland trail signage all meant to give the final touches towards the 'visitor' experience and set the area alight for a 'must come to venue'. Which was fine until that was towards the middle of the scheme and the bold suggestion we open and actually operate the railway for the coming high-summer season.

"Open?" A stunned silence followed. The Board of Directors had never envisaged that the railway would have to 'open'. The dream had been operating for so many, many years that none of the head honchos had really seriously considered actually 'operating' a real narrow-gauge railway for actual customers. Eleanor, she of the flowered dresses, gave out a long groan. An indication she was not pleased. "It is part and parcel of the grants that the project becomes a 'business and takes on employees'. That is why we received £250,000 in the process towards paying for it all." Another long silence followed. Eventually the Chairman thought he should break the silence. "Duw,duw,yes. But – are we rrready?" Ready, coming or not. The thought flashed through my head. Anyone would think we were playing a game of 'hide and seek'."It's a terrrible risk you know. People. English people. Forrreigners. All walking about. Asking questions. And the litter? What about the litter?" I didn't want to follow Eleanor's groan or bury my head in my arms to stifle any additional anguished cries. Instead I raised my hand which was bound to attract the Chairman's attention. His eyebrows shot up eagerly. "Shall I put the kettle on?" The Chairman could see he had been saved by the bell. His eyes brightened with appreciation as he nodded. A short break, a cup of tea, a biscuit and movements around the floor amongst a multitude of mutterings, would inevitably give the dissenters time to readjust to the new realities and allay the fears and the dread of finally having to go 'commercial' - at long last. – And so-sometime later- that was finally decided upon.

A re-enactment. Close inspection shows the new boarded end of the 'Loco-shed' in background.

'A Foray into Fortunes'.

The hazy surface of the stone ballast fused into focus before the fluttering vision in my left eye. Why was I lying alongside the track-bed? Then I remembered. I should have known better. –Don't go near 'starting handles'. They are not good for one's health. 'Sholto' the 'Huson Hunslet' diesel locomotive with the Second World War Ailsa Craig engine wasn't furnished with an automatic starter and required 'swinging' -with a handle. I weighed in at eight stone. The handle weighed in at three stone and the kick-back from the engines pistons weighed in at ten stone. The old adage came back as I picked myself up from the ground. 'Don't fight battles whereby you've no chance of winning.' I looked across my previous flight-path. The handle hung mockingly from within the engines ballast weights as if to say – 'Dozy pillock'. It wasn't wrong.

It was Sunday the 28th of July. The plan was to open and operate for six weeks until the 8th September. Only first I needed to start the engine. "Take the brakes off and give it a shove," suggested one of the four passengers due to travel on that first train of Wild West Wale's newly augmented 'tourist railway'. The customer was always right – only this time he wasn't. If by any chance I couldn't get aboard once it started rolling it would continue rolling faster and faster before ending up eighty foot down in the Celtic leet of the gorge one mile on and be lost forever, as were two ballast trucks from a previous 'scheme' some twelve months before. I looked around for a volunteer. No. Celtic gold would have been easier to find. Brawn was needed, not brains, and as usual it was never around when you needed it.

What I needed was Policy Jones who was good at swinging handles or a volunteer by the name of Chuck Hanks, otherwise known as Welfare, because he was a genius at obtaining it. He was the 'go to' man for all and any information regarding the Welfare State having lived off it for most of his adulthood years. Having reached the age of forty he could proudly boast he hadn't 'worked' (in an official capacity) a single day in his life. Strong as an ox he could carry two full length railway sleepers, one on each shoulder, and run a marathon at one and the same time. But he did have a 'very bad back' - - - !

Twenty one passenger journeys per day. One every twenty minutes. One passenger or thirty five, the capacity of the single attached passenger coach, it mattered not. A journey was a journey as the guards log specified. The little engine trundled back and forth on one gallon of diesel per day, excluding Sunday when Allan George, the Hunslet 0-4-0 slate quarry steam locomotive was proudly coupled in place following fisticuffs at dawn between the competing qualified steam engine drivers. "He had it the week before last," screamed Bella, one of the only two female steam operatives, "It's my turn – bastard."

"How about you take over for the afternoon shift?" I ventured cautiously. "What? -What? – Why don't you fuck off -!" I ducked as a cob of the finest grade black anthracite removed my hat and felled the white faced hapless footplate fireman waiting behind me. "You mad bitch -," howled the man holding up the offending article. "Have you any idea how much this stuff costs – bloody lunatic." He was correct. Steam coal was indeed 'black gold' which made Sunday running a very expensive occupation, not to mention dangerous to boot.

We were still completing Scheme Three which, by the close of the first week of passenger operations, I had managed to work out the knack of keeping the workers (and I use the term loosely) apart from the visitors. I anticipated a language problem. Not between Welsh and English but between good and bad. It was the only time I can recall pressing the lads to speak Welsh between themselves when in the vicinity of the 'incomers' until I realised that most of the bad words they used didn't have a Welsh translation. It was most disconcerting to see the faces as visitors listened to that beautiful, strangled throat language interspersed with harsh guttural Anglo-Saxon cursing and blasphemies every few seconds. Words which couldn't have been mistaken for anything other than what they were – foul.

I decided to tape-off the North-side nature trail and amphitheatre areas as work on the 'log-bog' and woodland pond was still in progress and confine the 'lads' to pond dredging by hand bucket for the duration. I should have known better. No-one actually drownded and contrary to opinion there was everything to laugh at on a regular basis – but the toll on lost wellies was enormous, so much so I threatened to send them into the water barefoot. "Yow must be fookni' jokin' -," growled Curly, coming up for air for the third time, " – yowd be 'andin' out douli hats next – an' changin' the peanuts t' rice balls." – "Bloody caper this -," his last words cutting off as he dived yet again for his left wellington super-glued somewhere deep in the glutinous mud of the pond's bottom.

'Déjà vue'. Strange how the brain works. Curly's last dive flashed a framed vision across my memory banks. We are back ten years. The pond is the size of a small lake in the spacious estate grounds of a 'Remould Tyre Baron' and the last job of the week to retrieve the oxygenation fountain lost somewhere out in the far middle. Things haven't been going well. We are in the throes of multiple bankruptcies. Two of our building companies having fallen foul of the 'property market' collapse of '74'. Harold, known as 'H', has secured the good graces of the major shareholder of what will become 'Quickfit' Tyre and Exhausts and the prospect of three major conversions of cotton mills to 'stack 'em high' stores are in the offering. Six months work. High profits but high risks. One of which would be to fail to find the man's precious solid stainless steel 'fountain' and reinstall it. We could of course hire a local 'frogman' complete with aqualung and bottles.

Which seemed logical to me as I squat down beside the lakes edge and peered intently into the still black waters below. "I can only find motor-grease," came the words breaking my concentration. "Put some on mi' back." I looked up, lost my balance, from what must have been the shock, and fell over sideways. 'H' weighed in at around 14 stone. He was naked, save for his underpants, wearing a bright red swimming mask, a green snorkel and a pair of bright pink and yellow flippers. "I've done t' rest -, he said waving around a can of axle-grease from which protruded a paint brush handle. "Do mi' back." Apparently 'H' has seen a programme on 'cross-channel swimming' and knew all about cold water and the consequent preparations thereof. It must have worked for he emerged ten minutes later in his same pearl-white skin colour carrying the sprinkler triumphantly above his head. One hour later and one gallon of petrol less, he again emerged from the garage, minus the axle-grease, but now a bright red from head to toe apart, so he claimed, from his bits and pieces which he maintained were dark blue. "Forgot about them," he mused. "D'ust think wife will notice?" - - - Would it have mattered I asked myself.

And here we are again. Ponds and lunatics. Who says history doesn't repeat itself!

The pond wasn't natural, unlike almost everything else surrounding it. Excavated some one hundred years previously by navies under the care of the Great Western Railway Co, those builders of this final three miles of branch line track-bed and bridges back in the 19th century. Leading in from the raised track-bed was one enormous 24 inch salt-glazed drain which collected all the surrounding forests surface rain water which was then dispensed out through a deep channel to somewhere off in the distance. Whence nobody knew and, as I wasn't inclined to put together a safari party of local marauders armed with machetes its destination has remained, to this day, unknown. 'Tree-huggers of the world untie'. I nearly got that right. When imagining a world of wooded countryside and forests one comes up with abundant swathes of delicate pathways interspersed with spreads of sweet smelling flora, the sunlight glinting through a canopy of gently floating leaves and the rustle of autumnal settlement beneath one's feet. Nothing could be further from the truth. Unfarmed woods and forests are almost impenetrable without the aid of chain-saws, axes, machetes and the odd flame-thrower. Even the wily fox rarely ventures forth against such obstacles. Pressed men will attempt penetration, given the right incentives. Volunteers usually have something wrong with them when the suggestion is made or they've suddenly forgotten a previous appointment elsewhere. Unfarmed forests die very slowly over hundreds of years. West Wales has clusters of them in spades. And this Welsh valley was no exception.

"We need a boat Boss," drawled Armourlite, he of the impenetrable brain. I instantly knew that behind the statement lay a kernel of commonsense. But for the moment it was passing me by. I decided on a different tack. "Righto. What size?" I replied. A blank interlude prevailed before -. "Bigger than a coracle Boss." It was to be hoped so. We had tractor tyres in the yard bigger than that. For a moment I toyed with the idea of a few planks and lashings then decided otherwise. I could do without any 'drownings' today.

The floor of the amphitheatre was knee deep. Forty tons of compacted shale had been replaced with a dark lake of water stretching from one end to the other and was, at that precise moment, lapping at the stage area whose wooden steps were threatening to sail away of their own accord. "T'is the drain bach. Blocked it is. Trrrickling so it is," There was nothing else for it. I sent for Curly. "Yow want what!" - - Taffy had tried roding the pipe with a 2" x 2" length of timber but to no avail. "Yow want me to crawl up there and poke about for a blockage?" I have to admit that is exactly what I wanted him to do, but I hadn't thought he would be daft enough. I was wrong. He was. The rope securing his ankles wasn't needed. When he found the blockage it obviously wasn't a happy blockage, given the force it propelled him back down the pipe and halfway across the swollen pond opposite. "Shit. Shit, shit, shit- !" he bellowed as he passed by executing a swift sideways crawl as half the forest emptied its mixed detritus in his direction. A finer display of drain clearing has never been seen this side of the Severn Barrage. The air was filled with a cacophony of gurgling and screeching noises as the surface of the amphitheatre suddenly took flights of an Irish 'river dance'. Thirty seconds later and the artificial lake had completely gone. "Hmm. That seems to be OK now." Very satisfactory I thought. Curly stared at me from behind a patch of pond reeds. I toyed with the idea of imagining what was going through his mind. Hmmm. - - Then thought, perhaps not -.

Our first tentative foray into the world of 'business' was coming to an end. Seven hundred and eighty two passengers plus three hundred and ten membership rides carried on six hundred and two passenger journeys. Not an outstanding average per journey but from small acorns – pigs have a whale of a time – do great oaks grow. With a total income of one thousand, four hundred and forty three pounds, a King's ransom on the societies normal monthly income, we, the four of us, myself, Johnnie Greybeard, Policy Jones and Welfare were lauded with glasses of Asti Spumanti, real champagne being thought too ostentatious, and awarded the grateful thanks of the railway company directors who paid for it from their own pockets. Planning began immediately for Bonfire Night, dreams of large entrance receipts and 'night-train operations'.

Great care had been taken to rope off the large stack of 'wood' in the centre of the yard. Everything was made in readiness for the torchlight parade as the executioner, Welfare, dragged the hapless Guy Fawkes (a dummy I might add) towards his impending doom, a burning in God's holy pyre. We dispensed with the hanging, the disembowelling and the long drawn-out process of quartering as there were small children present. "Duw, duw Mam. He's a bit limp isn't he? Has he been drrrinking?"- "Naw, naw cariad. He's not real. Symbolic isn't it." - "Symbolic? –What's symbolic?" – "It's - - it's - eat your welsh cake. They's going to burn him in a minute." - -"Aw, burn him. There's lovely." - - "Why?"

Went the night well. A thousand locals from all points of the compass, some having journeyed thirty miles or more and almost everyone having travelled on the valleys 'newest' tourist railway during the nights proceedings, all now gathered around the dying embers of the glowing bonfire for the great finale. - 'The Grand Fireworks Display'.

Welfare, still wearing his executioners black hood, didn't see the rocket coming as with a surprised look of consternation he discerned on my face I suddenly ducked out of sight. 'Whoosh'. The rocket drove into the crowd scattering all before it. "Fuck - - !" The curse was hardly out of Welfares mouth before a hail of brightly burning red balls exploded just above head height as panic broke out amongst the ranks of stunned spectators. It was then the whole top platform and the children's play-area lit up with three hundred fireworks all going off within a five second warfare assault flattening the front two rows of happy celebrators like a swath of newly mown corn-stalks. - Something had apparently gone wrong!

"It fell over." Policy Jones swayed from within the clouds of billowing smoke, hands and face blackened his corduroyed hippy trousers having melted into a bungle of wayward dangling threads. "A roman candle," he gasped. "It fell over – and one of the balls flew into the box." Mr Whiskers appeared from below the edge of the platform from where he had rapidly taken refuge and stroked lovingly at what was left of his smouldering beard. "The box?" Policy nodded. "Yes. The box." Mr Whiskers fumbled again with his beard. "Inside the box -! How did it get inside the box bach?" Mr Whiskers was going straight to the point. A bit like the remains of his beard. Policy picked gingerly at the melted plastics welded to his legs. "Did it open the lid?" Policy flashed his eyes which reflected the dark redness from the remains of the bonfire which against his blackened skin looked almost demonic. "Er - nope." –- "So - - - you left the display box – open?" Mr Whiskers didn't want to appear too accusing. Not with all the potential ramifications surrounding possible insurance claims or far-distant litigations that could possibly arise when the smoke finally cleared. It was at that moment Policy fainted. I felt like applauding. His timing was perfect. When in doubt, go for the sympathy vote. After all he was the village insurance broker and it was possible we hadn't been carrying any 'one-off public indemnity insurance' for that particular event. Fortunately nobody was seriously injured. We might have had to refund the more disgruntled or anyone with explosion burns but for now - the 'party' was over, the fire it flickered dull grey, we'd burst the pretty balloons and taken all the fun away – or at least Policy Jones has. All in under five minutes. – Now for the Santa Specials. - - - - What can possibly go wrong -?

Hail the passing - 1984. Welcome 1985 & A New Decade of Utter Confusion.

"But - -. But – you is English?" For a moment I was quite taken aback. 'Good Lord. Am I'! I wasn't aware the Welsh Republican Army had a race discrimination clause in its rules and regulations. Taffy took another long draw on his delicately rolled spliff and spun his eyeballs. A strained grimace crossed his face as lungs and will-power battled openly for ascendency. Willpower won. "Duw , duw Boss," he wheezed, I think they might find that very peculiar you'se being English like - - I could ask - - I suppose." I tried prodding-. "Tell them I could start as an associate member. Twelve months free trial – see how it goes." Taffy wobbled back on the tree stump on which he perched. "Trial -?" "Dearie me. Musn't use that word. Trrrial. They've only just gotten over the last one. Found not guilty they was. Innocent they was. Not a blem-ish. Couldn't get enough explosives you see. Detonator caps plenty but with nothing to stick 'em in. Not much of a 'conflagration' if you get my meaning. All 'puff' no 'bang'. Sad really." And at that the discussion on my recruitment to becoming a soldier for the National Free Wales Army came to an end. Not that it was serious to begin with.

The mysterious burning of three second-home holiday cottages on the North Wales coast had raised the interest of the less well intentioned throughout the valleys with hopes of yet another 'uprising' to cast off the colonial yoke of their evil bastard English occupiers. It was a sort of 'festival of futile hope' which came around each passing decade, striking fear into the local constabulary as Thomas the Terrorist, who was known to almost everyone, spent the summer months daubing quarry faces with red and green flag squares of 'Cymru Goch' (Red Wales) and posting threatening letters to local magistrates minus the official postage stamps. "They can tell from your spit you know." said Taffy - knowingly. It's the water you see. Local -. Isn't it." One had to marvel at this soothsaying prediction for at that time DNA could have only meant one thing, 'Diagnose Nothing At-all', given the first use of DNA, in Southern England for criminal cases didn't take place until four years later in 1988. It later transpired the cottage pyrotechnics was the work of the owners, English, who had conspired to defraud their home insurance companies. The planting of the Welsh flag a feeble attempt at diverting the local constabulary who knew full well no self-respecting nationalist would use the one bearing Llewellyn's red dragon or spend money on fast burning accelerants for that matter. "Local knowledge you sees bach, said Taffy tapping at his forehead in an effort to stop his eyeballs from spinning. "Local knowledge isn't it."

On a broader front the world also kept on spinning. In Northern Ireland it was the zenith of the real terrorists, The I.R.A. (Irish Republican Army) whose clandestine war blossomed into a series of bloody carnage whilst across the globe and minding their own business the environmentalists known as 'Green Peace' had their ocean-going flagship 'Rainbow Warrior' blown out of the water by a mindless 'cell' of French government assassins, in another futile bid to stop that movements annoying tactics. Pointless international piracy which served only to gain massive sympathy for the activist cause whilst wasting copious amounts of money as at the same time half the world's populations starved and the slightly better off contributed millions of dollars to 'Live Aid' rock concerts in aid of North Africa, Ethiopia in particular, who were losing millions of human beings to a disastrous famine and devastating ever-lasting decades of killer droughts.

At home quite the opposite was occurring. Water, water everywhere and the valley took on the appearance of a lake-land marina. We lost the river and our bottom field before Christmas and it didn't resurface until well after Easter by which time the otters, who had been sheltering in our chicken coop, found the incessant clucking too much for their delicate ears up and left the area completely. The horses however were pleased, for when summer came the new layer of river silt thus deposited produced a much needed abundance of lush green grass and somewhere for to take a good refreshing mud-roll.

"Bridge has gone." Mr Whiskers had that glum look on his face. "We is now going the wrong way boyo." Not wishing to add to his woes I did a smart tongue bite and refrained from saying "We always was." Going West had been decided long before my unfortunate arrival in Wales. I use the term 'unfortunate' very loosely for it really did have very many good points which I usually brushed aside. Going East had always been my preference given the longer distance, the more open valley and the many features of historical viewing that it afforded on the anticipated 'slow' train journeys, that 'could' have been. Now with the river bridge, minus one anchoring point, hanging drunkenly across its western span and the scalloping of massive indentations along its far bank by the river's floods, going West, added to the ranks of the 'dreams' when the £300,000 rebuild became apparent. It might as well have been three million. This section of Isambard Kingdom Brunel's Great Western Railway was no longer 'great' nor 'western' – and was going to be cut off in its prime long before it ever reached its intended destination. A bit like it was back in the 1890's when it was supposed to reach the nearby Irish Sea coast and failed miserably, by a good ten miles, having bankrupted its initial entrepreneurs, the Manchester & Milford Railway into the bargain – which it proved not to be. It now fell to yours truly, having volunteered, to make a further attempt westwards, to accomplish yet again, the impossible 'dream'.

"Who thinks a Baileys is a good idea?" There were thirty two members present in the room and immediately thirty hands shot into the air. Eleanor, she with the Masters degree, managed the merest of a smile. She turned and from the corner of her mouth whispered, "You need to tell them it's a bridge. They think you mean the whiskey liqueur." Only the chairman and his membership secretary had declined to vote. Them being 'chapel' as it were. The T.A. (Territorial Army) had offered to re-bridge the river, using the existing centre supports, free of charge with a second-hand 'Bailey Bridge' the only costs being the bridge itself. Hurrha! The cost of the bridge £58,000. Booo -! The railway could issue 'railway bonds' to raise the monies at a cost of £2,000. Hurrha! But we would need to sell a minimum of six thousand £10 bonds to clear the costs. Booo -! Everyone knew it was a non-starter. It took all year to sell six hundred raffle tickets and they were only ten pence each. It was beginning to look a bit like Christmas – all glitter and no gold. There also remained the reconstruction of the river bank. Hundreds of tons of meadowland had been scalloped away which would have to be piled and strengthened with gabions in order to maintain the support of the far side track-bed. A cloud of Welsh doom descended upon the proceedings - so it was decided to put the kettle on and have a think about it all. There was still another two miles of track-bed, not yet with 'track', to lay, which would take perhaps another two to three years to complete before the problem of 'no bridge' became a major priority. Meanwhile everyone should put their best efforts into finding an old 'mad person' with lots of money which, if successful, should more rapidly overcome the problem. Or at least ease the burden. Eleanor replaced her glasses with an exasperated sigh "I don't know why I bother. I really, really don't." I could have told her. It's 'dreamers' syndrome'. Sneaks up on a person. Insidious and all pervasive and it provides an innocent narcotic against all the other ills suffusing the planet. The civil war in Sri Lanka. The death of nearly two hundred people on a Zeebrugge ferry as it capsized and sank the other day and the loss of the last 'dusky seaside sparrow' which died that winter in Blackpool making its species well and truly extinct, just to mention a few. ---I was quite partial to a dusky seaside sparrow let me tell you. Bloody shame that.

We are still in the era of the 'Iron Lady' (Margaret Thatcher) – she of the 'not for turning'. We of the 'Good Life' fraternity have tried many ways to 'coin in' on this wave of 'change' or to put it another way, to 'avoid the jungle' that is the modern way of life -. Money -. Money is good. Money is life. Money is the new God. Society no longer exists. The upshot of which is the rich have slowly grown considerably richer and the poor considerably poorer. Everyone is to become a shareholder as the 'lady' destroyed the old and sold off the family silver with the slogan 'Tell Sid', whoever Sid was, with the inevitable end result that the majority of the nation's worth was snapped up by the big investors leaving the crumbs for the people to scrap and scrape over and share amongst themselves. Globalisation was coming in leaps and bounds. Self gratification in the form of 'free-trade' and 'just in time supply'. New technologies. New ways. New 'barons' for the 'new world'.

Meanwhile - - . She, the wife, or she who must at least be listened to, had tried opening a 'Bed & Breakfast' but found it wanting. That is 'wanting someone else to see to it all'. 'Riding Lessons' – we have the horses and the selection of gymkhana accoutrements – but the locals didn't want to seem to part with actual money. And so she had finally settled for returning to that in which she had been originally employed after leaving school – Banking. "Key Staff. It's part-time -," she said. Well of course it was. Everything was part-time hereabouts. It was to spread the jobs. Part-time was classed as employed making the three million unemployed look like one million. "So have yer got the keys then?" I asked hopefully, suppressing the vision of a quick entry and a flight to Venezuela where they didn't go in for extradition. "Fat chance," came the reply. Unable as they were to procure actual jobs the local 'Job Centre' had long ago settled that part-time or volunteer work was adequate for their needs – in that they needn't bother trying to find those thus categorised any worthwhile employment and as such meant they themselves could go home early to their own clandestine 'second jobs', to make their own ends meet. "T'is rural," said Mr Whiskers. "Countryside you see. Not many prrroper jobs. Supplementary they is. Very important. Every village has its 'Jones the Black'. I can put your name down if you want? But - - !" - - "Well. You is needed here isn't it. Bit of a mess if you isn't here. Runs better when you is." - - -"Fucked if you isn't -."

And that was about as near a compliment I was ever to receive from the organisation in what would later add up to a twenty two years of twenty-four/seven/fifty-two weeks continuous service. Personally I like to think of it as my 'lunacy period'. Ponder as I might I can come up with no alternate rational reason other than I had always thrown myself into my work caring little for other distractions – obsessive, workaholic – and as such it just came natural. I can say I thoroughly enjoyed it for the most part and have no regrets with any of it - - - well - - - almost anyway. There have been two major hiccups. The first in Ower town back in the day (see Ower Dabblings) and the second which is about to 'flower' like a rampant patch of limp dock weeds here in this ambient green of this peaceful West Wales valley.

"Solid oak kitchen furniture." beamed Braveheart, "Or better still solid Douglas Fir kitchen units in the classic style." For the past ten years Braveheart's riverside workshop had been producing antiques. Mainly of the Tudor Elizabethan period. "We should branch out." Indeed such would be a bold move. "Have you got any money?" he asked grinningly. I have to admit with that question the first thing flashing through my mind was tax inspectors, bank managers and fawning solicitors. Only creatures of that ilk had ever pervaded my space alongside that question.

Together, alongside second mortgages', we raised sufficient funds to enable a move to new premises comprising workshops and offices, a shop rental for the kitchen unit displays, all the woodworking machinery for a full scale production and enough capital for three months overheads. Meanwhile I was still managing the 'Railway' and looking for anyone remotely insane enough with the desire to take over such a responsibility. I eventually found him in the guise of the projects most favoured 'puffer-professor'. Richard of Whitland.

"You are going to die -." The words didn't make much sense. Apart from a few aches and pains, which had nothing to do with the railway or the wife or the damp weather, the lady doctor, who had spent ninety-five percent of the consultation time talking about her two miniature wire-haired dachshunds, smiled at me from behind her pince-nez glasses. "You have emphysema. You must stop smoking. Immediately. The report of your x-rays doesn't bode well for a long life. - - How many of the little darlings have you got now?" – What? – "When?" I heard myself ask. "What?" The pince-nezs' sparkled in the dim light of the file strewn doctor's surgery. "Oh! – Yes -. Ten years perhaps. - Are you thinking of breeding more?" I remember walking from her surgery in a bit of a daze. The words 'ten years perhaps' still ringing around inside my head. Ten years. Ten years. That would make me around my mid fifties. I remember thinking 'that's a bit of a bummer'. Ten years during which time I wanted to write a few books, get the railway up and running successfully and pay off the mortgage so as to leave my passing on the planet with a clean slate and

the family in reasonable good shape. Ten years - - -!
Perhaps - - -. Shit!

So when the offer of a new enterprise and a 'risk' of
making a pile or losing the lot came along in the guise
of the 'Braveheart' I did what I shouldn't have done
and said 'yes'. There are a number of sayings that one
comes across during one's lifetime. 'If it looks too
good it usually is'. 'Trust in no-one but yourself and
then only half trust yourself' and 'If someone tells you
they are a professional or an expert – get a second
and a third opinion'. All of which were appropriate
here. Nevertheless, throwing caution to the wind I
threw myself, wholeheartedly, with a diagnosed
limited future, into the fray and to hell with the
consequences. Kitchen World – solid wood - here I
come.

17th century pot-board Welsh dresser

with fully-boarded plate rack back.

A Braveheart 'make-up'.

'The Hitler Writings'.

From memory, it must have been around the summer of 1982, I received a telephone call from a 'friend' from earlier times. He went by the name of Charles Edward Broadstairs*. Fourteen years had since passed without even a postcard. Alarm bells rang. Chas never surfaced without he wanted something and it was usually dangerous. "Have you heard of the Hitler Diaries?" he said after at least five minutes of waffle and small talk. "No." I replied. "He didn't keep any diaries." To clarify the matter Chas knew of my lifetime interest with history and specifically that of the Second World War and the German's Nazi government. So much so that even the minutia of the people and the period I would have at my fingertips for any interested observer. "A friend tells me they've surfaced amongst a lot of other stuff, some of which is for sale. I was in Augsburg last month and I thought it might be worth looking into." Augsburg, Southern Germany. Yes. That certainly rang true. "I would be amazed, not to mention my flabber being gassted, if any such writings ever came to light." I replied. There was a pause then. "So you think they are bent?" "The disappointment in his voice was palpable. Chas had a voracious appetite for anything 'Nazi', specifically daggers and insignia and anything which may have been the private property of that man, Adolf Hitler. "Absolutely. I wouldn't touch them with a barge-pole if I was you. He didn't even write his own book Mein Kampf, Hess wrote it for him. He detested writing." From that the conversation turned again towards the mentioning of a few 'old' acquaintances before -. "Well it's been good to catch-up. You should come over and spend a week or two here. Beautiful place. Beats the crap out of 'Blighty'. Oh yes! By the way. That 'Hess' thing –" Another short pause then -. "You might be looking for a body in a cave – towards the end of the war, if you want a handle on it. – Ciao for now." The phone went dead. I thought no more about it. The barn was minus its roof after the heavy winter snow and a fresh batch of corrugated steel sheeting required my assistance to nail it in place. 'Hess' (Deputy Fuehrer of the Third Reich) would have to wait. The goats were getting wet.

 It was to be eight years later before that particular snippet of information came to have a far more important meaning. When it did it settled once and for all my prevarications and negative reasons on the writing of the books. And me with a mark of 4/100 for English Literature! – He said, our English master, it was because I had spelt my name right. Barsteward.

*(For Chas.E. Broadstairs see- Ower Detinue or Atlas D.Four -Scripts on Black).

It is the spring of 1990 and all's well with the world and as usual when everything is under control – the wheels fall off. HTV (Harlech TeleVision) have procured a short documentary from YTV (Yorkshire TeleVision) from their magazine programme 'Calendar' entitled 'Ingleborough- the body in the pothole'. It tells the story of a body discovered at the end of the war in a pot-hole going by the name of Trow Gill and an accompanying suitcase with some very strange contents. I knew immediately this was what 'Chas' had been referring to in that last conversation. Why he couldn't have told me of its location and subsequent investigation that followed, which because of his background he invariably knew, I couldn't fathom. But that was 'Chas'. Everything on a need to know basis – information is power. Now was the time to turf my daughter from her roof-space bedroom, which she hadn't used since its construction some four years previously, and resurrect my writing desk and open those files which had lain dormant since our arrival in Wales some ten years previously. Pencil to paper. The computer had yet to arrive this side of 'Offer's Dike'. I was short of only one thing. Time. Where to find the time? According to the wisdom of my own local medical professional I had little under ten years left -!

As those who have self-inflicted upon themselves reading the previous books in my story will be aware, I rarely do things by half. More often it's diced much more liberally. I had forsaken my home town and all my previous mad-cap endeavours of 24/7/52 work-table for a better more leisurely existence. Yet here I was again piling on the pressures of too many irons in the fire. As director and overseer of the railway I was expected to attend daily for a couple of hours and quite often twice a week nightly for the plethora of 'meetings' of the various departments. As director of the new company with Braveheart and the kitchen suppliers I was to fulfil a six day week at our display salesroom (a small main street shop in the local town) and, in my leisure time, be at home where my family, livestock and 'books' constantly demanded my attention, the whole of which to be properly 'settled' and 'viable' within the next tumultuous decade.

"You're obviously a prat boyo." – - Was that a voice in my head or had I dreamt it? I looked around. Mr Whiskers appeared from behind one of the railway carriages. "I'm beginning to think those English have put something in the water." I studied the remark. Being English one does. "It's Welsh water. Say's so on the meter by the front gate. Dwr Cymru." Mr Whiskers pulled at his bobble. "Duw, duw bach. We knows that. But they's all English that does it isn't it. Otherwise why would they sell it to Birmingham – and at such a low price see you. No,no they's English. Definitely." I smiled, as one does. So why did that make me a prat? "It's Policy you see. Not happy he isn't. He is talking about resigning he is – and his wife, Gaynor, talking about cancelling their memberships. It's Richard you see. Driving them mad he is. I told you he would. He's a school caretaker. Bricks and mortar. Not people. He's not a people person. Desks. Blackboards. Chalk. Mop buckets – this -," he waved a hand across the open yard, " – this is beyond him bach."

Richard of Whitland had managed just the one season before his lack of holding things together crashed into oblivion on his prevaricating indecisive fumblings. He wasn't management material. Although to be fair to him he had made that same remark when he accepted the position some twelve months previously. He left. Without a blemish on his record. The odd derailment, mis-felling of a giant oak tree, the loss of a couple of despairing members and lack of regular bookkeeping never appeared in the company's reference when he signed on at the Employment Exchange. He was a nice lad was Richard and one needed to be kind to such rare specimens of our species. They are few and far between.

 "Then in that case I suggest you let 'Policy Jones' and his troubled wife take over the present day to day management seeing as how they think they can do it so much better. I can't. I already have far too much to do as it is." Mr Whiskers took a long stroke of his beard, which had fortunately grown back following the 'night of the wayward fireworks'. The corner of his eyes wrinkled into a satisfied grin. "There's clever isn't it -, he said very, very slowly. "No wonder they call you 'Hitler'. Divide and conquer is it?" Hitler! That's a turn up for the book. For a moment or two I was at a loss for words. I had never considered myself to be in that much maligned league. I knew a very great deal about the man and could see no comparison with myself whatsoever. I decided to let the remark go. Nothing comprehensible could be gained from going down that road. Not at the moment anyway.

Through the mist: Pencil and paper.

Excerpt from 'Black Dove' -1990.

Hitler knew Hess was pursuing a meeting with British contacts and warned Hess not to become too complacent or too embroiled else he get his fingers burnt. – 3rd of May 1941 at the Reich Chancellery in Berlin.

Hitler did not know Hess had been in contact with Sir Samuel Hoare in Spain – 26th April 1941. Nor did he know Hess planned to fly to Scotland or anywhere else on British territory. Had he have done so he would have strictly forbidden it.

 Albert and Martin Bormann were the only ones of the Nazi hierarchy to know of the true destination of Hess. However when Martin Bormann tries to speak to Hitler of the Hess negotiations he is told quite bluntly to keep his nose out of the affair and ' not concern himself with the Deputy Führer's agenda's'. This does not mean Hitler knew anything other or more than what Hess had already told him.

*   *   *

Contrary to suggestions made, Hess never intended to land his plane, Bf 110D, des. VJ-OQ, on the runway at Dungavel House, Lanarkshire, in the dark. The runway was a small grass strip more suited to Hurricanes, Spits and Lysanders, although it would have been possible for a pilot experienced in night flying, which Hess was not. The runway had landing lights but these were rarely if ever used. If on the 10th May 1941 the runway lights had been switched on, the purpose was clearly as an indicator for Hess, a guiding beacon, by which he could parachute down near to the house and not for landing purposes as has been suggested. Furthermore, if a 'reception party' had been awaiting Hess's arrival at Dungavel House, as has been suggested in other quarters, then of Polish/MI6 origins most certainly but not including the Duke of Kent or the Duke of Hamilton.

Hess fully expected to be taken directly to the Duke of Hamilton upon his arrival at Dungavel. This had been arranged through his meeting with Hoare in Spain. Movements recorded at Dungavel on the night of the 10th May are (as far as is known) of Polish origins. The first man to interview Hess was the Polish Consul from Glasgow. This talk was held in German without interpreters present. No one else knew what was being said. These coincidences reek of SIS involvement.

No wonder MI5 howled in indignation when they discovered Hess had been interviewed prior to their arrival on the scene.

Churchill half expected the arrival in this country of at least one of the Nazi hierarchy in response to the 'M' sting. He was not surprised and neither was his private secretary when informed of Hess's landing. Hence the remarks: Churchill – "So the worm is in the barrel." And Coleville's remark of "Has someone come?" before being told of anyone's arrival from across the Channel. What was meant was that the 'virus' had worked. At least one of the 'idiots' had fallen for the ploy.

Hess was not murdered (at that time) or replaced by a 'double'. He was however kept incognito to stop him from talking, as it were, 'out of turn'. It is when the war in Europe is over and Hess was returned to Germany to stand trial for 'war crimes' at Nuremberg that the problems of keeping him quiet arose.

Hess was warned he was not to speak with anyone about anything that happened between the years 1935 to 1945. The warning was made all the clearer with him on trial for his life and the possible dangers to his family now under allied protection. The promise of a life sentence as opposed to the death sentence for his part in the Nazi's crimes prior to his 'peace' mission was a sufficient inducement.

When it became apparent that as an old man Hess could no longer be kept in a prison cell – due in the most part to political pressures from the Russians who never believed the British 'explanation' of the Hess mission and to a mounting public pressure in Germany, Rudolf Hess was finally eliminated. He was silenced, murdered, in his prison rooms by those who wished his knowledge to die with him. As it did. But not his papers or the SIS reports of the time. The most important document in this whole affair is the original letter from the Duke of Kent to the German Government in the winter of 1940/41.

 In the early summer of 1945, King George V1 sent his faithful MI5 servant Anthony Blunt to the Hess Estate to retrieve all personal correspondence he could lay his hands on.

Blunt, with his usual flair, did just that and under the noses of the Americans, in whose zone the estate lay, and who were unaware of the true purpose of his mission. Frau Hess, under the impression she was assisting her husband's case, was more than accommodating and gave Blunt everything he asked for. All these papers Blunt returned to the Royal family (and possibly copies to his masters, MI5 & the KGB with whom he was also employed). Thus are we given the secrets of the 'Hess Mission' the secrets so carefully hidden from the public's gaze since 1941. - - Why - - ? Reputations. Nothing more. Nothing less.

An intelligence 'sting' perpetrated by the British SIS on the Nazi Government, brilliantly executed but of which the world cannot be told for fear of its misinterpretation and for fear of the exposure of those 'well heeled' great men and good who at a time of this country's most darkest and dangerous hour were quite prepared to 'deal away' this country's freedoms and those of our European neighbours'. Hess knew of them. That was the problem. And still is.*(See Black Masquerade & Black Dove. Same author. *

Apologies Dear Reader –I seem to have gone off track . Let's return to more present day memories and leave the dirty secrets of yesteryear to long lost others:- However just as a reminder I will leave this here:-

Scripts on Black by Atlas D'four.

'The Glorious Nineties'.

Glorious in that they cast aside the grotesque maladministration's of the socialists versus the capitalists desires for power and the bitter consequences that ensued for the majority of the working people. Glorious in the feeling a new dawn was breaking as the century crawled towards an ignominious ending. It would never rank high, as did the '60's, but short of another world war anything had to be better than the past two decades.

It began with a recession. Great. Just what was needed as we put the final touches to the new shop premises, the factory and the financing for a new outlet in England in one of the more wealthy prominent stock-broker belts of the 'home counties'. The last quarter returns of '89' reached just above £25,000 which by the second quarter of '90' had fallen to £12,300 and still falling. Break even was around £10,500. Which surprise, surprise we managed to skirt by in the last quarter of that year.

"We won't last another twelve months if this carries on -." I went to great pains to convey my misgivings to Braveheart. Bank overdrafts of £90,000 at seven percent were not my idea of fun when the work was draining away faster than the lamenting wails of a ragman's trumpet.

"Starless and bible black. Down to the sloeblack, crowblack, fishboat bobbing sea." - -"We need to do better-!" - - "T'is the sales you see." said Mike our local shop and sales manager. I turned towards him. The desire to throttle him on the spot welled up. One more quote from his half-mad drunkard of a Welsh idol Dylan Thomas and I would remind him he was the firm's salesperson by shoving a solid wooden love spoon up his large expanse of an over-used posterior. "You don't fucking say - - ." Was the best I could offer at that moment. To make matters worse not a single order had come through from the new shop following the Christmas grand opening. Not even a plate rack or a welsh dresser which the three lads at the factory had turned over to producing with the almost total collapse of the kitchen unit department. Shades of bankruptcy, yet again, loomed before my eyes but this time I had my whole life in the creditors hands. Last time it had been easier to save sufficient to continue. Not here in the wilds of West Wales. When the cowboys came to town this time around they would be carrying flaming torches and lynching ropes and when the bankers (I nearly got that right) had finished there wouldn't be enough assets left around to shake a stick at. My previous references to Hitler at this time seem to be very poignant for the scene near the close of the 'business' – late 1992 – were reminiscent of the final days in Hitler's Berlin bunker. At the factory and the shop in the Home Counties the employees, having been made redundant at the behest of the liquidators, partied away their final hours on copious amounts of beer and vodka. In the office above the shop here at home in the market square, a despairing Braveheart had completely lost it. The 'devil may care' and 'tomorrow is another day' was taking a day off.

"Ruined? Fucking ruined? I am undone. Screwed. Knackered. How could you let me become so?" I was hoping he hadn't meant me? It wasn't my idea. I had suggested a completely different enterprise, albeit even more fanciful at the time, and one that wouldn't have necessitated almost mortgaging everything including the wife's knickers. I parried the accusing wail. "It's just bad luck. It happens. We began on the wings of a 'boom' and got nailed by a sudden 'bust'. Perhaps we should have seen it coming. But we didn't. That's life!"

Admittedly I had been in these circumstances before and therefore wasn't as upset. "What are we going to do? Where do we go from here - ?The questions, those, and a dozen more, came fast and furious as Braveheart sank lower and lower into the folds of the Victorian captains chair behind the long oak desk his grey ashen face drooping at every torturous wail. I was just thankful he wasn't in possession of a Walther PK .38 pistol or a cyanide capsule.

 Explaining to his ever suffering wife why he wouldn't be home that day, or ever again, wasn't something I would have cherished – let me tell you. Shirley Braveheart was a dead shot with a soggy dishcloth not to mention her set of boomerang horseshoes she kept by the front door. Why at the front door -? Believe me. You don't want to know.

So in the summer of 1992 I returned again to the railway – but this time instead of payment by criticism and meaningless platitudes I demanded and not surprisingly got actual money. A living wage, even if it was for pigmy people. Policy Jones and his part-time bookkeeper wife had left taking their memberships' with them. There was a vacancy that had to be filled. So who better to fill it than the one who had overseen and managed the building thereof and its nursery years as a tourism destination. Atlas rides again – dearie me! And here's me thinking I was smart.

The nineteen nineties were to be the railway's best and glorious years. Built upon the crumbling foundations of dreams and little monies its final outcome seemed doomed. But for the present and still accommodating its caucus of well-intentioned 'puffer-nutters' and willing volunteers, by the middle of the decade it was the talk of the valley. 1994 saw the centenary of 'Alan George' its gleaming little tank-engine and a celebration of over three thousand visitors in less than one week. There followed a number of smaller special events in the guise of 'telethon's' for 'Live Aid' and various charitable causes including the BBC's Blue Peter and two sunny seasons in the woodland amphitheatre featuring a 30 piece orchestra and a plethora of wandering medieval players. Rail-track extensions continued apace until the line finally reached the river and the drooping bridge. Two and a half miles at a leisurely ten miles an hour and a timetable of one train per hour carrying a potential 100 passengers per journey. What could possibly go wrong! - - -

'Summer 1994. Victorian Day. Alan George sits astride the level crossing with yours truly in Edwardian costume sporting the straw boater'.

In the middle of the summer the bailiffs arrived. Our little house on the hill and all its attendant land and buildings were required by the 'banks'. Again it was the best of times and the worst of times. Best because one of the things I was good at was going well and worst because I was now homeless, along with a family and a herd of livestock. To make matters even worse I was still alive and feeling remarkably well. My doctor had died. Alcohol by all accounts. – We should pause at this juncture and read that last paragraph again -. Here I offer humanity some advice -.

'Trust in no-one but yourself and then – only half trust yourself'.

Our new abode nestled in the dip of the river in a near-by village that went by the name of 'Tree-Grows' – an English version of its Welsh name which only a true Welshman could pronounce. The cottage and the land was rented and at a price half the cost of our previous mortgage. 'She who must at least be listened to' made all the arrangements without complaint or recrimination. That, dear reader, is what one calls a good companion and wife and goes in the file of the 'best' of times. For once I had made a good choice and in that - a very lucky man.

Life on the railway wasn't without its humorous side. 'Laugh' – we didn't know when to begin. I must have been doing a good job as the visitor numbers doubled then trebled to reach a figure commensurate with a number of our competitor railways of a similar size. Yet our volunteer base remained stagnant.

As with all volunteer organizations people come and people go. Turnover in this little Welsh valley was akin to Piccadilly station. Or at least so it seemed at the time. Some might last the day. Some a week and some a month or two and some you couldn't get rid of if you tried. It is to the latter I most solemnly dedicate this book.

They came in many categories. Social. Curious. Scrounging. Charitable. Obsessive and the worst of all the narcissistic megalomaniac with the 'cunning plans' by which to infuse confusion and hatred amongst the very few long suffering dedicated followers.

I came to detest the meetings whereby the phrase – 'No. What we should do is this –' sprang forth from new members whose tenure was but a week or two old but whose advices would be eagerly gathered up by others who were at a despairing loss themselves of how to improve the railways all pervasive and constant tenuous existence.

'Follow my Leader' or better still encourage him from the sidelines, where it was less dangerous, became a regular feature as the years rolled on. Being responsible but with no actual power to properly control outcomes is not, from experience, a very rational place to be. I know. I was there. And tolerance, for those so inclined, is needed in spades. Allow me to demonstrate -.

A good manager delegates. He knows his selection to be sound and of warranted choice – always and given there is a choice. But with a volunteer force never exceeding half a dozen most of my 'choices' were grasped from the winds. When asking for volunteers, one finds all the line steps backwards, it's more a case of 'owt is better than nowt'. If someone actually stepped forwards there was an immediate buzz of muted comments, usually of the suspicion variety.

'Billy the Barkeep' had stepped forward. That seasons entertainments in the woodland amphitheatre required booking. Seven night-time Wednesday performances in July and August. Billy was awarded the position of 'Entertainments Manager' on the usual salary of 'minus sanity' and sent forth to accomplish his worthy task. I didn't have to wait long.

"How much"! I thought at first he was reciting the band's telephone number.

"Three hundred and sixty pounds - - that's with ten percent off," he replied his grin of satisfied accomplishment slowly sliding from behind his bearded chin. "That's cheap that is. It's usually five hundred for them. They's well known in Aberystwyth." - - "Aberystwyth? What! Aber-bloody-ystwyth?- Are they known in bloody London?" Billy had to think about that before -."Er no. I don't think so." " Why not? For that sort of 'bunce' they should be known in New York as well." I hissed. "And Tokyo and Paris and bloody Istanbul. Cancel them."

Billy's features froze. "Cancel! I can't. I've signed the contracts," he said giving a rapid twitch of both eyebrows. "Contracts! You've signed contracts? When?" "Er – last week." "Last week -! Last bloody - - !" By now I had run out of incredulity. My next phase would have to be one of grovelling damage limitation.

In all Billy the Barkeep had signed away three and a half thousand pound in fees. Almost twice the annual budget for the summer entertainments. His repost was he hadn't been given a budget. My repost could have been that he also hadn't been given a brain. But one doesn't do that when the devil drives and 'assistance' is as rare as hens teeth. If all went well the monies could be recouped. As it transpired July and August proved to be a wash-out.

Only two performances took place with a loss to the railway of most of the fees plus threats of court action for those cancellations I managed to secure. And such instances as above recorded were not unusual when faced with willing volunteers just passing through, as most did. Billy the Barkeep (so named as he ran a small hostelry in a nearby village) stayed a member of the railway for a number of years but was never again given any complicated tasks. The railway just couldn't afford such luxuries. Although there was always those who thought it could.

The 19th century Signal Box which arrived dismantled and remained in an overgrown bramble strewn disarray for over ten years. Transportation costs £800. Finally erected at a further cost of £1,100. Looks good. – Finally.

Three Standard Gauge passenger coaches. Purchase price £1. Transportation costs £1,300. Never renovated. Sold off as scrap seven years later.

Four partially dismantled Standard Gauge locomotives. Cost Zero. Disputed ownership. Recovered by bailiffs of the court nine years later.

Crane Gantry 10 ton Max. Cost £500. Erected and never used. Dismantled for scrap 15 years later.

Tunnel Toad Wagon. Cost zero. Renovations £1,500. Utilized as miniature museum for 5 years. Removed 14 years later for use as a farm shed.

Charcoal Burners (industrial). Brand new. Never used, Costs £1,200. Sold ten years later £200.

Just a very, very small sample of the regular antics of the willing volunteers who made up most of the committees personnel. A lack of proper disciplines brought about by the lack of a constantly fettered management through a constitution that brooked no force majeure. Or as someone once said : A cockamamie 'tail wagging the dog' enterprise. –

Seems fair enough to me.

For once by a stroke of good luck and lots of form filling the railway society was awarded a Heritage Lottery Grant for the purchase of another narrow-gauge quarry locomotive on the basis it was being offered to buyers in Japan and being 'Welsh' in origins it should remain here in Wales.

Kerr-Stuart Mfc.   'Sergeant Murphy'   0-6-0T. 1918.

'Old Soldiers Never Die'.

Three years in the making. Three hours to be destroyed. Such was the dedication and loyalties amongst the railways membership as the old guard slipped silently away through age and decrepitude and the new guard took up a fleeting but very troublesome residence. A sort of 'steam enthusiast handy-man'. Lots of talking, very little doing and knowledgeable about everything from a gunge flange to brain surgery. What the new generation 'puffer-nutter' actually knew could be written on the head of a pin whilst still leaving space for a signature. Not that at first glance one would have known it. He (and quite often) she, having dispensed with the previous two hundred years of railway knowledge, would regale anyone willing to listen to the 'modern' way of thinking. Which more often than not bordered closely with 'OO model railway' and a perverted version of Thomas the Tank Engine. It was obvious that as the century waned so to had the 'age of steam' and with it the willingly dedicated railway building enthusiast. "Well boyo. That was very informative-." Mr Whiskers comment at the end of the two hour 'Presentation'. "But I doubt your audience understood what you was getting at -. Seemed a bit baffled to me, especially when you went on about income and expenditure. Their eyes. Sort of glazed over. Catatonic they was. Spaced out like."

To cut a long story short. Around the middle of the decade I had decided to 'clue up' my sparse knowledge of tourism and its business in Wales and obtained a degree with a three year course at the nearest university college the results of which I now felt the 'project' might benefit from. Hence my presentation. Twenty years had passed since the new rescued railways inception. Most of which with it balanced upon a knives edge and a foreseeable closure. Ten years of operations had done nothing to remove the danger but the business was now attracting sufficient public interest as to remedy that fact. Always and providing the right moves were made and soon. For the past three years and after months of cajoling the powers that be in Cardiff for grant assistance, I had formed the valley's first tourism consortium. The printing and distribution of a half a million leaflets to three hundred potential tourist venues across West Wales and beyond which, according to survey, boosted the valley's footfall by an average of twenty percent per annum.

That, coupled with the railways first ever profitable annual returns – yes we actually made a profit, albeit miniscule – and the thirty plus thousand visitors that year prompted me to believe there might actually be a future for a permanent well-balanced business and even more outrageous thoughts that the railway members might also feel likewise. Dreams dear reader – dreams. When hell freezes over more like.

Eleanor, she of the masters degree and flower patterned dress, may have had some sympathy for me. Where it not for the fact she had been 'banned' again for exceeding her remit. It transpired she had been thinking, on her own. Then doing things, on her own. And keeping things secret, on her own. Her latest expulsion would turn out to be a ten year ban. I looked forward to the day when it would be my turn if only to get some peace. After twelve years voluntary I was now three years in pocket with a living wage salary. There was still some distance to make up as things stood.

The project hovered on a cusp – and a very tenuous cusp it was. Some wanted a tourist attraction with 'Kiss Me Quick' hats and candy floss. Some wanted a steam heritage attraction with a limited single aspect outcome. Some wanted a private diesel-engine club, 'members only' and some wanted a social club with 'Cheese & Wine' and 'Bridge' nights. I might add that the majority wanted stuffing but that would have closed the gates for good. Which was never out of the question and might well have been the ideal answer to it all had it not cost getting on for a half a million pounds over the past twenty years and far more what its present sale value was worth. The 'books' said £340,000. But that was on a basis of housing on site by modern-day prices. I thought I'd better think it out again.

Some will have heard of the 'Night of the Long Knives'. Where the railway was concerned it went one better by extending them to weeks. My advice to the constant small trickle of new volunteers was simple. Stay out of the politics. The quickest way to lose one's faith in the organization was to become 'involved' and the quickest way to agonizingly up-sticks for less stressful climes. One years tenure was considered remarkable. Anything longer and one stood in line for the Nobel Prize for Steam – the Wheel-tapper & Shunters Ten-pointed Star. Over five years one was easily considered as unredeemable and lost to useful society, which put me down in the mummified section for posterity to discover during the end of the climate change in the years leading up to twenty second millennium. The old man (my father) always said I was a problem – qui – moi!

"Do you wish to call a 'Major Incident'? asked the voice on the other end of the telephone. I paused -. Did I? "Well – it could be – I suppose." I replied. "Thank you caller. Please stay on the line." "I can't stay on the line. I need to get there -." It was no use. The wheels of the emergency services had sprung into action and the telephone lines to the nation's acute public assistance had been flung into unstoppable mode. - -What had I done!

It began with the locomotive's fireman falling headlong through the door wheezing heavily having run over two mile up the railway track, and gasping the words –. " The engine – she's off the - track. They – need – assistance!" -before collapsing in a tangled heap at my feet. Had he or anyone else bothered to tell me he suffered from asthma I might have reacted differently. "What the fuck -!" I grabbed him by the collar. "Are the coaches off as well?" The man's eyes glazed over. "Dunno.- Dunno -." he croaked, his eye lids fluttered a warning of – I'm about to faint. Go away and stop strangling me. "O shit." I let go of his head. Perhaps if it bounced a couple of times on the wooden floor he might just begin to make some sense. He didn't. So it was then I telephoned the emergency services. Bad it must be for him to have run all that way in that present un-nerving condition.

 The midway section of the railway track went by the name of Llandyferiog and stood on the slopes of a hillside escarpment. The land either side angled sharply downwards and was covered in a tall green carpet of high bracken and bramble. Advancing upwards, with only their yellow helmets showing and bobbing erratically up and down like piston-rods, came the local volunteer fire-brigade. One white helmet, obviously more important than the rest, broke through the curtain of fronds at my feet.

"Code Red is it bach -?" wheezed the ruddy puffed out face expectantly. Just then the passengers grouped along the trackside broke into applause. A signal of appreciation at the great effort the rescue squad had made. I waited for the applause to die down. "Well – er –no –er – not exactly." The man heaved himself onto the fence wire putting the last final strain on the century old post wooden alongside which promptly snapped in protest. "Duw, duw. No Code Red -! Red you know. Blood. We was expecting casu-alities. Fatalities -. Lots of them-." The fire-chief looked around. "A fire perhaps?" I shook my head. "No sorry." By then the ambulances had arrived. Three with sirens wailing. "Code Black. We had a Code Black." exclaimed the first of the para-medics tripping over the broken fence in his haste to be helpful. I was about to explain again when the police cars arrived their blue lights flashing and above my head the humming rattle as two dragon-fly type helicopters hove into view. " We've had a Code Blue Rescue One. Who called a Code Blue?" hissed the Fire-chiefs radio. "Do you have casualties Rescue One. Over." The Fire Chief ran his eyes along the bunch of civilians who now full out of feelings of gratitude all now with cameras out clicking away briskly at the blue sky above trying to get an action shot. "Negative Humming Bird One. Looks like a very dry run," replied the Fire Chief attempting to smile at me at the same time. I stood my ground and removed my hat which I slowly inspected by running my fist around its interior before replacing it. "Well you see - -. It was like this - ." I began - - .The Fire Chief took his leave of the anticipated scene of a catastrophic disaster as 'Sholto' the little Ailsa Craig (1942) diesel locomotive arrived to rescue the passengers and re-rail the steam locomotive. "Don't worry -," he said, "It's all good practice for the teams." All the other emergency service vehicles and their personnel had already left. "Some of them get lazy. Very few disasters in this neck of the woods. I could strangle some at times. Doesn't do any harm to shake them up a bit." I know how he felt. There was one particular fireman, responsible for the de-railing of the engine by splitting the points, and for being incoherent with message-carrying, who might yet get strangled before the day was out. Not being religious I cast about for something to 'give me strength' - - and decided a fag would have to do.

They do say it's an ill wind -! The passenger figures for the rest of June doubled. Everyone wanted a ride on the –Disaster Averted Railway -. The headline in the local newspaper of 'Near Fatal Disaster' and a photograph of my smiling fireman holding up an inhaler for all the world to see galvanized the more macabre and ghoulish, along with their wailing offspring, to - - ride on the 'near death railway' just for the thrilling experience - -.

And today Atlas you will be The Fat Controller! What! You find the thinnest person on the planet and you really think he can portray Thomas the Tank Engine's main human character? My cheeks, the only time they ever look full, puffed out in exasperation. "There you is." said Mr Whiskers. You can do it when you tries."

In an effort to stay with the times and entice a good Bank Holiday clientele the 'society' became hell-bent on raising the railway's profile with an offering from the Reverend Audrey's children books. 'A Weekend with Thomas the Tank'. The entertainments committee was allocated a budget of two thousand pounds, although when it came to 'allocating' nobody knew who was on that committee and what's more nobody wanted to own up either. It fell back on the previously named who it transpired were no longer alive or who had long departed to hound some other unlucky heritage railway elsewhere.

"How much!" - - I thought there must be some mistake. "Twelve hundred and fifty pounds for the two day license and twenty five percent of the ticket revenues or a lump sum up front of five hundred pounds." came the muted reply. I jotted the figures down on one of the café serviettes. "And what do we get for that?" Billy the Barkeep brushed his forefinger rapidly up and down his grey moustache. " A fuckin' headache'?" - he surmised with an exaggerated lift of both eyebrows.

For once I had to agree. It would be unlikely the two days rail ticket revenue would exceed fifteen hundred pounds with profits from other enterprises bringing in another five hundred. "And what do they do for that sort of money?" Billy moved to stroking his goatee whilst he pondered. "Well - - - ." "Yes I am thank you." I replied. "Or at least I was until a few seconds ago." "Well –." he continued. "We get a Thomas the Tank face for the locomotive and lots of Thomas the Tank Engine and friends paraphernalia and permission to - - - er -- go broke I suppose." - - And so yet another bright idea fortunately bit the dust before yet another 'off the shoulder' suggestion dwindled the coffers towards a situation ever more dire than usual. I was learning to treat all and every suggestion percolating upwards from the various consortiums and committees with extreme scepticism for as I discovered almost none profited the railway or bode it well- or at least, to my knowledge, not so far this century.

"You toot yer horn." Chuck Welfare, he of unintended violence and long standing, looked at me askance. "Yer do what?" "You toot. On the way down. Two toots – one – two – toots. That way he knows to be trackside when you come up." Chuck took in the information slowly and rolled it around his spacious cranium. I could see the information was for remaining, albeit only for a short period, but long enough to ensure he understood the precise instruction.

Richard of Whitland was 'the' longest supporting member still active amongst us having been at the projects inception in 1972. Already enthused by the magic of steam the mere thought of rescuing one of Beeching's axed rail-routes was more than he could rationally avoid. What Richard didn't know about railway soakaways, drains and regulations wouldn't be worth recording for posterity. His department, which consisted of himself, was Permanent Way & Trackside, which required trackside maintenance sheds every five hundred yards to 'house' his 'mountain' of tools and various forms of equipment plus accessories for every trade in Christendom. All I might add supplied initially from within his own pocket. He would arrive at the crack of dawn leaving his intended whereabouts on a scrap of paper and instructions as to what time he was to be 'picked up' later in the day - - with two toots of the locomotives whistle."He wasn't there Boss." "Who wasn't?" "Richard." "Did yer toot?" "Yea. On the way down like yer said and again on the way back." "How many times did yer toot?" "On the way down and on the way back. Twice." "Did yer toot twice on the way down?" "Yea – and on the way back." "So you tooted twice on the way down and twice on the way back?" "Er – no. I only tooted twice – like yer said." - - So now I'm beginning to lose the will to live. "So - - yer tooted once on the way down and once on the way back?" - -. Chuck threw his head to side. "Er - - Did I?"

Richard was a stickler for railway regulations. The 'rule book' was carried by every person on site who was involved with railway operations at all times, without fail. Being caught without your 'rule book' was a 'sackable' offence. Not that there was anyone to 'sack'. Had I taken that to heart there would have been nobody left to operate the place. "We exist by virtue of a Light Railway Order by dint of an Act of Parliament 1979. The 'rules' are laid down in writing. We are a Statutory Authority in our own right and as such are duty bound to observe the rules at all times." said Richard, at almost every meeting every month, year in, year out. I knew instantly what the problem was. One toot from Chuck's whistle would have been ignored, regardless of the correct timing. Richard only heard one toot which could have signified squirrels on the track or the fireman losing his balance from a bout of coughing due to snorting coal-dust. Such was the way of things. No –two toots. No reaction. "Then you had better uncouple the carriages and go back down light engine." I said peering intently over the rim of my glasses. "And this time –Two toots as you are arriving -. In fact. Just stop trackside. Pick him up and reverse track -. Can you do that?" Again I observed the space fill up with the words. - - - Yes. Good. But would they stay there and, mores' to the point, - - for how long?

'The Best laid Plans - -.'

To all intents and purposes the forthcoming decade promised, historically, to be full of 'eastern promise'. The city had got over its jitters following the collapse of the 'pound' and its dalliance with the ERM and the political ground seemed willing to accept the new boy on the block 'Little Boy Blair' – come blow up your horn the sheep in the meadow the cows in the corn –.' We, the sheep, obligingly grazing whilst the cows, the power-mongers again took another pregnant opportunity to grab and cosset everything of value around us. Nevertheless – life had to go on.

It was time to take another one of my famous risks. We had dallied too long with indecision and in what 'sphere' the business should be operating.

Ever since we officially opened in 1985 I had instituted an annual census on the 'visitors' through surveys of one kind or another with such questions as 'from whence do you come', 'where are you staying', 'how did you discover the railway', 'how was your visit – tick 1 – 10, 10 being very good' all in a tick-box format (one didn't want to over-tax a temporarily resting brain) and 'would you recommend us to your friends?', etc etc.

Compilations over the years had proven very useful to direct advertising and make additions to the venue in accordance with some of the customer suggestions – whilst disregarding the odd comment offered from 'Disgruntled of Mapplethorpe' or 'Pissed off from Poole'. Believe me when I tell you, there is always 'one'. Experience had told me that one satisfied customer will tell their friends, perhaps two or three others. But one dissatisfied customer wants to tell the whole world and his wife, as loudly and as disingenuously as he can to exaggerate his pain.

A business plan was prepared, put to the Board of Directors and decided upon. A five year plan of cautious expansion. A nucleus of paid employees, in order to guarantee adequate manning of all departments, three permanent and six part-time or as we say in the trade 'seasonal'. Staff uniforms with the railways crest emblazoned thereon and a franchising of both café and shop on an adequate rental return, thus relieving yours truly of their administrative burden. With the valley marketing consortium in full spate it was all hands to the pumps. - - So to speak.

A through breakdown of the required budgets revealed a break-even point of fifteen thousand visitors per annum, some five thousand less than the average for the past three years. What could possibly go wrong! - -I know. I know – I keep saying that don't I.

The oil tanker hit the rocks at dawn punching a very large hole in its front starboard hold and began to spill its cargo of crude oil into the Irish Sea at a humongous unstoppable rate. Ooops! There go the beaches and that seasons visitors. Two years later the people of Wales decided they could govern themselves much better than the National Parliament in London and voted for autonomy which resulted in Welsh Office grants being suspended and not replaced – again - . Ooops! Both would have a significant effect on the railway's trading and ability to function safely from a business point of view. But do we want to go there?

So much for the best laid plans of mice and men and just when you thought it was safe to go into the water -! I did seem to pick my moments.

"Good morning, good morning, good morning – how are we all today - welcome to the railway. Have you been before? – No. Dearie me, how remiss of you. All the same family are we? – Splendid -. Are all these children yours? Yes! Lovely. Have you discovered yet what is causing it? - Super. Here's a welcome leaflet. The next train leaves in a quarter of an hour. Have a nice visit."

Boldwyn, she of the ample chest, having directed the visitors and their vehicles to the appropriate parking space, retraced her steps back across the yard for the next batch of unsuspecting arrivals. This could be the start of something new. Customer Service.

"The customer is always right - - even when they are wrong." The three part-time 'welcome host wannabees' looked at me blankly. "Unless they poke you in the eye with their fists." Siobhan, her of Irish extraction, raised a finger -. "Ah t' be sure and what are we t' do den -? "Duck." I replied. "Unless you're daft enough to let them smack you one." It was arranged for everything to work like clockwork. Only I suspect this 'clock' had been made in Russia. Siobhan always seemed to be at the gate when nobody was arriving and halfway across the yard or in the engine sheds when they were. What she wasn't supposed to do was leap out from behind the 'Tourist Information Centre' (a large wooden shed) swinging her leaflet bag like a banshee screaming –"Slow down you tick English bastard." - - "You need a welcome leaflet." - - Still – it was early days.

By removing the four seats in the rear of carriage No.1 and some smooth carpentry work we formed a 'mini bar'. Under the Railways Act it wasn't necessary for the selling of alcohol on the train to require a license – always and providing the 'vehicle' was transportable i.e. that it could move.

The railway carriages however lacked corridors although most possessed a middle aisle. It wasn't so much the selling of 'booze' as finding suitable volunteers to staff it. Billy the Barkeep put up his hand, only as rumour had it he had already drunk his way to bankruptcy in three of his previous pubs, so that was a non-starter. Also finding a safe place to put the stock every night in order to keep the local children from stealing it. I felt like a squirrel does when hiding its winter nuts – Ooo, how about here? Ooo how about there? Ooo how about we pack it all in. It's driving me nuts- never mind the bloody squirrel. It seemed no matter how clever at secreting the stock we were, the little barstewards always seemed to find it. And talking of bar-stewards. We eventually discovered our weekend bar-steward had a younger brother and together the 'rewards for his loose lips' was serving them both too well. He wasn't so much fired as buffer-hauled when the truth finally came out. We did however operate the 'bar' very successfully for a number of seasons before the problems of manning and the Welsh chapel teetotallers managed to kill it stone dead. Another little earner sacrificed on the altar of 'dreams'.

The next good idea at the time, was a size smaller railway -. " Much smaller and the passengers will be bigger than the engine," grunted Esme sarcastically, she of the Quality Street gang with a farm, a footman and plenty of room for a herd of Welsh Pit ponies.

"There are fifteen different size railway gauges. At the moment we posses two – this will make three." Richard piped up, letting drop another pearl of railway wisdom. "How much will it cost?" "About nineteen thousand pounds." I replied. At the far end of the table Big Mike, treasurer for that year, fell off his stool. He needn't have bothered. He was always doing it. Had I said just nineteen pounds the reaction would have been the same. However this time he did seem to tarry a tad while longer under the table. Robbie Ridgeback, the Chief Engineer and Responsible Person quickly offered to reduce the final figure by a thousand or two with the use of his own personal JCB – to cut across the hillside and reduce the angle upon which the new miniature track would be operating. "You mean it will have to go uphill?" The look of incredulity on Esme's perfectly modelled face made her false eyelashes fan forward like the spreading of a randy male peacock's tail. "It's not a problem over 1 in 50, on a short run and in reasonable weather." Richard again, he could be invaluable sometimes. Esme withdrew her eyelashes together with that weeks plan to scupper the possible improvements to the railways progress. There would many other opportunities to come. Esme liked to keep the 'pan' boiling otherwise –what was the point of it all and - where was the fun?

"Where's the train –?" Everyone thought his name was Edward. It wasn't. 'Fat Eddy', he of the sailor's gait and wave motion, swayed onto the new platform eyes bulging from the exertions of his panic-stricken run from the tree line two hundred yards away. "It's still on the track." he wheezed. I breathed a sigh of relief. At least this didn't seem like another telephone call out for a 'major incident'. "So what's the problem?" – "He's unconscious," – "Who's unconscious?" – "The bloody driver. He hit a tree." I knew Chuck, he of unintended violence, was prone to accidents but this seemed just a little far-fetched. "What with!" Fat Eddy had to think about that one. "His head – I suppose," he replied, still swaying on the spot. "But there aren't any trees within half a dozen yards of the track." I growled, knowing full well that to be the case. Fat Eddy pursed his lips, "He's er – he's not on the track. He's at the bottom of the hillside." The reply wasn't what I expected. "What the hell is he doing at the bottom of the hillside attacking bloody trees? He's supposed to be driving the bloody train?" Eddy drew in a full lung of air -. "He er – he fell off boss." – "He fell off - - ?" Eddy smiled. "Yea. I know he did. Sideways. Woa – bang. He must have somersaulted half a dozen times before he hit the tree. Good job he did otherwise he would have ended up in the yard alongside engineering and Robbie Ridgeback's caravan. You know what he's like about our lot going down there." - - - And so began our 'Green Dragon' half-a-mile, two engine, four carriage, nine-inch miniature railway resplendent in its new Great Western painted engine cum maintenance shed and platform with its 'new all weather picnic area covering' and new antique Tunnel Toad museum for the use of -. The company treasurer had resigned three months previously when the costs had rapidly surpassed the twenty thousand pound mark. I've never seen a man so distraught -. But then Big Mike had never been the stuff of 'new horizons'. Model Mike, he of a less moribund stature than his predecessor and obsessed with anything of a '00' gauge, took over, his school teacher background eminently unsuited for financial wizardry which seemed lost where value for money was concerned. He obviously hadn't been in charge of any school but he was used to large expenditure figures. As to its origins -? Wasn't that someone else's problem? – I will just leave that there whilst you ruminate on it.

Change in a city entrepreneurial organization is often frowned upon but change in a rural setting is almost tantamount to a cardinal sin. Or to put it in a more familiar phrase –They don't like it up 'em'. To go from a 'go-lucky (I won't say happy) existence' to one of organized disciplined intent, was far more than some could bear. Whilst the employees made every effort, money being the imperative, many of the volunteers greatly lacked any willing compliance.

The older end, otherwise classed as the 'puffer-nutters' had always dressed for the occasion. Johnnie Greybeard never failed to appear resplendent in his GWR Guards outfit whilst accompanying Robbie Ridgeback in his bowler hat, waistcoat and polka-dot sweat scarf which he wore whilst steam-engine driver. (For the diesel engines he lacked any such respect, a flat cap had to do). But beyond that the rest looked to all intents and purpose like itinerant navies. I suspect many did so in order not to be waylaid by milling, half-brain dead visitors, as some called them. "If any bugger asks me 'where the bloody toilets are' again I will bloody scream." growled Sid from Swansea, although he was a Northerner and who had only come for an hour to paint the platform railings. "Three miles West. In the town. On the bloody Market Square -. Bloody tits!" In addition there were of course a number who thought the railway should run on a part-time basis without paid employees and thus resented giving their time 'free' – generally from the social and heritage camps. The Board of Directors simply wanted everyone to get along with each other and stop the incessant squabbling. As for yours truly, I was smack bang in the middle. On a policy now of paying for a nucleus of staffing the 'open season' ran for eight months. In the closed season, New Year to Easter, we prepared for the next years visitors ostensibly making annual repairs and urgent maintenance together with fresh marketing and other new promotions – as and when sufficient volunteers deigned to appear through the muck and grime of the winter weather. Talk about 'trials and tribulations' -.

"There's a cracked rail just beyond Pont and all them bloody fishplates haven't been off in the last five years." Sid from Swansea and his illustrious mate Raffe (real name Ralph but we won't go into that now) were holding a 'council of displeasure'. Going off the black looks I was receiving I used my 'get-out clause'. "I can't interfere with engineering. It's not my department." I replied, hoping to slink away quietly. No such luck. "Well who is?" snarled Sid. "The Board of Directors." I replied. Raffe, who held one of the directorships, looked off into the distance, probably unaware such was the case which wasn't unusual as many only paid lip-service to such responsibilities. Sid gave a snort. "This place is a bloody joke -." I change tack -. "Where's Robbie?" Raffe returned from his foray with the distant skyline. "Probably bonking 'Helpful Annie from Abergavenny'. Last seen, the pair of them, going into his caravan two hours ago. It hasn't stop vibrating since." I smiled one of my best of facial innocence. "That's not my department either -." I said, before quickly taking my leave for more salubrious climes.
Togetherness was only an aspiration as the constant struggle to meld ice and fire took up most of my battled-scarred working days.

'Pennerallt Boeth'*

Six dogs, two cats, a friendly rat, three horses and two offspring took up too much space on the grassless pocket-handkerchief size lawn at 'Tree Grows' and when the wife, she who at least must be listened to, complained, my suggestion we have the two kids adopted met with a blackened disapproving scowl. - So we moved.

A fourteen acre smallholding on the hillside edge of town and previously a fruit & veg market-garden production unit - named as above*. The owners, whom I ever recall seeing just the once, had decided to go 'sailing' –for about ten years. I suspect it was to 'disappear' considering the obscene state which their property, upon our arrival, was in. The 'Wreck of the Hesperus' sprang to mind with the addition of the 'The Rape of Nanking' to boot. I can honestly say I have never, and will never again, see a piece of beautiful countryside so carelessly and badly treated if I lived throughout three lifetimes. We would live at the property for eight years by which, at the end of that period, I had managed to return the land, upon which it stood, to some semblance of order and respectability. Rural vandalism isn't just practiced by those who hail from the urban conurbations. Not by a long way.

The two long poly-tunnels had the appearance of a 'stop-frame slow-action movie scene'. Colanders' have fewer holes. It was like a ticker-tape parade in instant replay mode. Full of jagged tears and patches and in a high wind - - . I toyed, only for a second or two, with replacing the polyurethane sheeting then opted for the least troublesome answer. Use the least damaged areas and forget the rest. It was never going to add to the beauty of the place. Six loose boxes and a food storage area. In the adjoining field stood half an acre of gooseberry bushes and beyond that what had been an acre or more of vegetable plantings, as the grassed over furrows irritatingly displayed. Which left four other fields surrounding the whole in which for the horses to graze. Given such manna from heaven she, who at least must be listened to, found two more horses that needed her loving care and attention and promptly demanded more loose boxes – just in case.

The obviously deceased tractor had a fourteen foot elderberry tree growing up through its steering wheel. Why? "Perhaps to stop it being stolen." suggested Ower Sean, he of the teenage years and permanently glazed over expression. "No," ventured his mother. "It's so you can climb up easily to pick the flowers or the berries –I think?" Barmy. The pair of them. I'm sure it's not me! Then again. One never knows. West Wales has some weird effects if one tarries too long -.

"This is Jamie -!" I was being presented to my daughter's latest choice of partner. "He's got a bad back." I was inclined to enquire was there anything else wrong with him as a 'bad back' might only indicate he was an idle bastard, but going off his cement stained appearance and obviously weathered features instantly gave him away as from the 'construction' fraternity. I know. I was there. The calloused handshake only served to confirm it. "He has his own house top of the village." – Well now. That was a step up. I already have two grandchildren, boys, from her previous attempt at 'togetherness'. He, Craig an industrious local youth of a sensible nature, had been six years older at the time they disappeared from my presence with –"They've got a flat the other side of the valley-." as I was informed by, she who must always be listened to, one Sunday evening in the middle of dinner. Spitting out a lump of home-grown cauliflower I followed through with –"But she's only sixteen! What the hell is she thinking?" "She's seventeen and she's reasonably sensible. Or hadn't you noticed," came the retort. To be fair, I hadn't.

As a father I could possibly score a mark of four out of ten. It wasn't that I didn't like children, I could most certainly never eat a whole one, but being of an obsessive nature with a propensity for absorbing myself in whatever project I had initiated myself in at the time, didn't lend itself to fatherhood or for that matter good husbandry.

As for animals, I quite liked dogs, had a brush with horses and saw almost everything else as the delicious contents of a pot roast. But I did possess an agreeable nature – most of the time. I think -? Delving on and much further into the future those two male grandchildren, a trait from my side of the family, expanded to five, all boys, thus exposing myself as a traitor to the traditions by having produced a female along the lineage. Her demeanour was likewise from my side as she took after her grandmother, my old lady, with the ability to carve her adversaries asunder with just one deadly glance and a propensity for throwing things like knives, pumpkins, kitchen chairs or whatever came to hand at the precise moment of annoyance. Her previous partner had drawn the line when she attempted to throw him bodily out after him slapping her in frustration. Both agreed it was no longer worth the bruises. So with that well known phrase 'if at first you don't succeed try perching like a budgie' I'm presented with a new chap with a Scottish name, a Southern English accent speaking fluent Welsh with his own house and no room even for a hamster. But each to his own I say - - - . Life must move on - - .

The farmhouse, originally of the 'long-house' variety, was built of shale-stone but with a relatively new slate roof. Warm in winter and cool in summer. It was served by its own private spring water, intermittently pumped from a catchment well lower down the hillside, hidden in amongst a small copse of woodland. It worked better after I fished out two dead mice and what might have been the sad remains of a hedgehog. It certainly made the coffee taste better. Situated just below the crest of the barely sloping hillside and sheltered from the prevailing winds the lime-washed walls gave out a panorama of apple green at the rear to a brilliant eyeball numbing white across the frontage in the bright summer sunshine. Fortunately such days were limited – even though the 'Gulf Stream' did wash upon the distant shore some ten miles west. And there was room to swing more than the one cat. It was certainly worth the rental price as she, who must at least be listened to, was at pains to retort. "That's the price of a 'box-cupboard' in London. On our money it's the best we can do." The 'key-staff' job at the bank was no more. The bank having decided something called 'the digital age' was about to unleash itself from the wilds of California. Now she took her educated qualifications, two GCE's and a 'well at least you tried' pass to the local petrol station where her superior knowledge was immediately recognized, regardless of the fact she couldn't speak Welsh, and where the proprietor was beside himself at the wonderful depth of her understanding English. "Well you see our people, they get confused doesn't they. It's the trrran-salation. English to Welsh to English to Welsh. It's the brain you see. Takes time. Annoys the customers when they's

English isn't it? All that thinking - - and they want it doing straight away doesn't they?" - - - "Are you used, each week, to a lot of money." - - - "I only pays the normal - very weekly." The proprietor, friends of ours, grinned. Just his little joke. It hadn't fazed the wife. She was used to it. The jokes and the little money. A job's a job when all's said and done. - Alongside the farmhouse stood a Dutch barn. Inside, where the hay should have been stored and covered in forty years of dust, sat a Ford Standard with flat tyres and no steering wheel and probably worth at that time, in that condition, some ten thousand pounds. The landlord had made a point about wanting to remove it. But meanwhile I should keep an eye on it. After our first delivery of hay it hardly mattered. It couldn't be seen anyway. Perhaps as well as 'farm thefts' were rife in the area. An old classic car wouldn't have been a problem given the 'sleight of hand' hereabouts.

From around the adjoining fields it was obvious the owners had had little time for any real 'land management'. Ragwort, deadly to horses in its dried form, nettles and large clumps of 'dock' nestled in abundance. A goats' paradise as some might say. Not again. The last time goats have been used as weed vacuum cleaners at the railway I spent endless hours rescuing various one's from self-inflicted self-strangulation or chasing escapees down the line until they fell over in confusion. The horses would just have to manage.

Déjà vu. --It was on the breeze. Not being one for spiritual leanings, being taken from the doorstep on a lonely Welsh hillside to the fringes of a huge pine forest on the banks of the Detroit Canal alongside Lake Eyre, was fractionally mind-boggling. It is dusk. Twilight. Suddenly the air is filled by the rustling of a million leaves. A white mass, a mile wide, rises from amongst the tall pines like a ghostly apparition. It glides in unison towards where we are berthed. Our ship is damaged and lies in quarantine awaiting parts to be flown from Germany. We sit motionless as the cloud, which I think might be condensation, creeps steadily forward. I realize it is making for me or at least the ship on which I am standing. Being just eighteen years old I'm not convinced it wants me personally – but that doesn't stop its onward motions or my imagination which by now is running rampant. To make matters worse no-one is allowed to leave the ship. It hovers. The rustling noise increasing in volume. Suddenly the noise stops. It descends as one. At the same moment I realise my mouth is wide open, my jaw having sagged towards my chest. "What the - - -." In less than three seconds the ship turned white apart that is from me, although I'm not usually any other pallor. Even the steel hawsers hugging the ship to the quayside shone like strips of taught bed linen. I looked down at my feet. Moths. Millions and millions of moths. Every steel part of the ship was covered in them as if somebody had passed over the superstructure with a paint spraygun. Somehow they had missed me although I think one had tried to crawl into my mouth as they jostled for position. "You're too cool Peggy." smiled the ship's cook. I swaggered, as one does at that age, "Tell me about it Cookie." – Heat. The very thing upon which living things thrive. The moths had left their daytime sunbathing as the night drew in seeking warmth through the long hours of darkness. Metal retains the heat from the day and it was to this their nature was drawn. Survival comes in many forms. None more so than in this North American wilderness. - - - - And all from one whiff of the evening's breeze - - -.

Our nearest pine forest was half a mile away on the steepest part of the hill and if it harboured white moths it was news to me. To be on the safe side I gave it a glance anyway. Nope. Not even a murmur. Apart from the animals and the wife and kids the only thing that followed me to these wild hilltop climes where the debts, some many tens of thousands. 'Blood out of a stone' springs to mind. Never a borrower or a lender be, saith the Big Book, as both shall suffer outrageous fortunes. For the second time in my wandering span of life, so was it to be. Zilch, as the Hebrew might say. Or if from my neck of the woods -. "Tek the 'airs owt er that one fella," as the odd Bailiff or two would discover as they slunk away with no luck and no commission either. One even had the bare-face affront to offer me a Jehovah's Witness pamphlet – hopefully, –. Bloody Hypocritical Tit.

'Operation Rusty Rail-spike'.

For three years the 'five year plan' operated successfully as the staff settled into a regular routine. Even I was surprised that the usual mumblings and grumblings from the volunteer departments seemed to be few and further between. Sod's Law it wouldn't last.

Jealousies, personalities and the lust for 'power' inevitably burst through the seams of the camouflaged balm with a particularly 'slow' season as the millennium approached and my decision to cut down the winter season salaries for the five permanent staff, myself included, to which the Board of Directors had unanimously agreed

However, this limited company limited itself to appearing infrequently at board meetings and accepting the rulings of its shareholders through their custodian trustees under the constant threat of the 'Board's' dismissal. In other words they always negated any absolute control preferring to accept the 'will of the people' against the 'good of the company' – with all its constant consequential disasters. The Tail that wagged the Dog.

 "If he refuses. Throw him off the bridge." The Chief Trustees instruction to the would-be conspirators came as no surprise.

Eight years previously when the then Chief Engineer had refused to work voluntarily, my instructions were to 'sack him and throw him in the river'. Mansell-Jones, Lord of the Manor and head-honcho of the 'Salmon & Trout Association' had a propensity of throwing people in all manner of directions, which I suspect came from his ancestry when the 'robber-barons' ruled the countryside and the rule of law barely existed. It would appear I hadn't been the last person to speak to him. Whether or not that had been intentional, as I was probably passed caring, I really can't say, for such was the man's major failing, but it was to have the conspirators' desired effect. They wanted me gone and I'm not sure I gave a damn – even though it would only add, big time, to my present financial problems, not that anyone other than creditors would give a toss about that either."You have to hand your keys over -!" said Robbie Ridgeback thrusting out an upturned palm. Helpful Annie from Abergavenny, his trusty co-conspirator, leered expectantly over his shoulder. I stared back, but not with any humour. I had been expecting some trouble for some time. "If I knew of anyone in the organisation who had the qualifications or the expertise to run the place I would." I replied. Robbie scowled. "Mansell-Jones says you have to give them to me," I couldn't resist the opening -. "Does he know you're bone idle and semi-illiterate and a piss-poor man-manager to boot? Or does he believe the tripe in that fraudulent CV you've been hawking around to various other railways recently?" The look of surprise on the Chief Engineers face would have graced a Tate Gallery masterpiece. "Did you think I didn't know?" I hadn't been the manager of the railway for sixteen years, given for one short break, and not been on familiar terms with numerous others in the same business. "Does he know you spend half your time here watching television and the other half bonking your fair maiden-." Abergavenny Annie ducked away from my pointed finger as if it were a loaded pistol-. " – Or did you fill his head with another wagon-load of bullshit, like you usually do?" My sudden rise from behind the desk prompted the man to stagger backwards crushing his 'grease-monkey', she of the loose womanhood, up against the metal coat hooks of the office door. Her muffled screams were cut short by my delicate form of dismissal. "Fuck off you pair of useless pillocks." Admittedly I hadn't bothered to refine the words to any great degree. But then I had been rather busy with the latest VAT returns, just one item no-one else there, at that time, could understand never mind complete and send off. I sat down slowly and stared at the hurriedly retreating backs as the two 'wanabees' fumbled themselves from the office their angry voices muttering garbled obscenities in their wake. There was to be an AGM of the Society and the Company later that month. Only the Board of Directors could 'legally' fire me as I worked, under contract, for the Company. Although I harboured no illusions as to their wishes to be involved or make any such gargantuan decisions such as that. That really would be asking too much. Previously and during the intervening weeks the railway membership had risen sharply, coming as a surprise to everyone. A further twenty or more potential volunteers, many from other railways, and changes to 'Standing Orders' had been adopted to enable them to take full advantage of their annual fee – by giving each individual the right to vote from their date of joining. It should have rung alarm bells. But it hadn't. It was called 'back-loading' So come, in that month, the Annual General Meeting of the Society all rotational directorships were filled by new members instead of the old incumbents retaining their 'seats'. Robbie Ridgewell may not have been a very good Chief Engineer but he did make a good Chief Hatchet Man when it came to messing up the inner workings of a railway society. The new Board of Directors, half of whom didn't actually know me, acquiesced with the Custodian Trustees wishes and offered a 'pay-off' of my contract of employment for my 'silence' and 'exclusion', which I took, and if I am being truthful, not reluctantly. It was the end (so I thought) of a twenty plus year relationship. I had managed the construction from the bare bones and moulded it, as much as I was allowed, into a 'break-even', reasonably efficient organisation that with care and attention could, with the right financial interest, go on to greater things. But somehow I doubted it. Was there that much 'luck' here in the Wilds of Western Wales. If there was I had yet to find it.

Back on the 'ranch' I now had the opportunity to throw myself into 'cleaning the place up'. I began by removing the elderberry tree from the tractor and replacing large areas of polythene sheeting for the 'tunnels' with a plastic, more durable, woven tarpaulins, something the five horses certainly appreciated. It was then I also decided it was time to re-write the 'books' whose pencil and hand-written manuscripts I had hawked from the 'old town' and moved from hay-loft to stair-cupboard over the past twenty years. She, who must at least be listened to, frowned as I uncovered my small electric typewriter from under a cloud of dust. "According to the television, publishers are only accepting floppy discs for submissions. Paper manuscripts are out." she said. I frowned. Well it was my turn, "Oh - really – are you sure!" Her face wrinkled. "No. Not at all. I just thought there was a little too much oxygen in the room and I decided to use some of it up," she growled. - - - -. I suppose I asked for that

The computer arrived the following week. So we looked at it for a little while, had a cup of tea and then looked at it again. My enquiry had what might have been best described as a dumb ring to it. "Where are the instructions?" She, the font of all domestic wisdom, peered around the back of it.

"There aren't any. I've got a little man coming -." Fortunately that didn't mean she was pregnant again. "- and your son has been doing IT studies at school in his last form." We backed away. We had no wish to manhandle the machine any further. Although it looked like a television and was the size of a television and plugged in like a television it most definitely wasn't a television. It had no 'channel' buttons for a start and no aerial socket. "Well it's no good askin' me. The nearest we ever got to a maths calculator was a slate board, a piece of chalk – and some maniac wielding a big stick." She, who must at least be listened to, gave me one of her loving smiles. "Well at least you have the satisfaction of knowing they wasted their time petal -." Cheeky cow. "Wasted mine as well." I retorted. I took another long look at the tall box alongside the 'TV' with all the slots and buttons and things protruding from it. It was obviously electrical because it had a plug on it. "Er - -What's a floppy disc- -?" Too late -. Her retreating back. Horse feeding time. I knew my place. I should have to wait in line. I peered closely at the box again. Nope - - and I bet it was made in Taiwan.

My first attempt at publishing I like to call my prequel period. After numerous rejections from the many publishing houses I eventually discovered a lesser known house given the name 'Remainder Publishing' (little did I know how prophetic that nom de plume was likely to be).

Throwing caution to the wind I allowed them to 'put together' my first offering from the 'Ower Kid' series, which for a small fee, sold fifty three copies in its first week, and none ever since. It didn't fall into the category of 'vanity' publishing more a question of 'futile'. It was a good lesson for the learning and thankfully I hadn't used the words 'Ower' in its title. I haven't read it since less it bring on my latent PTSD. The period was slowly approaching when I would expect sadly to lose both my parents which in itself one wishes will never happen, but which I also knew would give me carte-blanche to be truly honest with any autobiographical tome I might wish to unleash upon an unsuspecting world. Ower Kid, my brother, would have to take his chances. He has a gammy leg in his old age and can no longer catch me. I had intended to write two non-fiction books on World War Two and three largely revamped autobiographies. I ended up writing ten books on the Second World War and five autobiographies and finally, after another publisher that went bust during the process, succeeded in obtaining a publisher who was prepared to take me on merit. This time the whole were published, over a ten year period, before he also went bankrupt. And the moral of the story is – stay away from publishers and publishing unless you already have celebrity status or you're a sad corrupt politician. Then you are assured of a 'best seller'.

They say the loneliest occupation is that of one who is a 'writer'. I know of a few lighthouse keepers that would scorn such a claim. Given my life, as laid out for the whole world to see, one might be inclined to think I would be the last person to abide alongside such an occupation? And you would be wrong. Gregarious and slightly hedonistic is my public persona. Solitude and quiet is my inner persona. Both I can do equally well. Writing had never been a great effort, which given my school reports would have come as a great shock, especially to the 'old lady' and the majority of my 'teachers'. But again we won't go there as again it could possibly trigger off my PTSD and in consequence drastically deplete my wine store. (See Ower Darkling etc).

And so we pass my parents century, the bloodiest in the world's history, for the new millennium and hold our breath for the world's computers to crash into oblivion alongside economic mayhem and utter devastation, better known at the time as the 'Millennium Bug'. Ooops! No that didn't happen either. The credo 'Greed is Good' reigned across the planet as the rich grew richer and the poor grew rice. If they were lucky.- - - Ah well. Alas. Back to the drawing board-.

'Civilisation Cometh'.

The caravan had long since lost any virtue for its existence. It stood on a concrete plinth opposite the farmhouse and had been home for the owner for a number of years whilst the farmhouse underwent a major renovation. Windowless and almost floorless it had served as a dumping ground for anything and everything that would fit through its narrow doorway. So much so it was, in places, impenetrable.

The letter informing us it was time to 'move' arrived in the Spring of 2004. Time for a 'pow-wow'. The previous day one of the young foals had almost decapitated me by lashing out with its hindquarters, fortunately at chest height, and depositing me twenty feet away amongst a patch of nettles. Had I been female I would now be tit-less. Instead two neatly imprinted roundels, slowly turning black, supplanted my nipples. "I'm gettin' too old fer this." I ventured, hoping that it might foster some common-sense. "I think we should be looking to settle for something less arduous and with just a dog and a cat." Zoo time, for me, was coming to an end. Many decades had passed since those heady days on horseback amongst the windswept mountains of ower Northern hills where as young lovers it had seemed it would never end and a 'fall' would be laughed at as one bounced uninjured off the tufted moors spongy surface.

It was more 'splat' and 'crack' and flashing blue lights if one had the misfortune to fall off one's horse now. She, who must at least be listened to, threw me a glance, which was better than the knife she was dicing the potatoes with. I did tend to pick my moments. So far so good. I would try again later.

"The brake is the one in the middle – dickhead." "I know it is," my son retorted indignantly. "Then why is your bloody foot on the accelerator." Ower Sean, he who isn't joining, looked askance, then at his foot before gently removing its resting place on the offending pedal. The squeal of the engine's pistons running berserk ceased. We both turned our heads and peered through the low windscreen of the Morris Mini to ascertained how much longer it would take for the man in the car we had just hit to fall from his driving seat onto the road. It would have been an easy operation for he no longer had a door keeping him in. Ower Sean had seen to that. When the man straightened up I felt a guilty glow of satisfaction. Had my son chosen better I would have demanded he go and buy a lottery ticket that same afternoon. It was the bank manager, the one who suggested a larger tranche of borrowings, then administrators and then foreclosure against the administrators' written recommendations. "Whatever he says deny it all and don't admit liability. He hit you – even though he didn't. We can let the insurance companies sort it out." I purred in a low voice.

"But - - ." he was about to protest. I gave him one of the 'old lady's', his grandmother's, glances, which said if you wish to die keep talking. He knew better. Whose suggestion it was that I teach him to drive I don't remember. Not that he should have needed it. He had been driving since he was fourteen years old. Mainly motocross and drag racing. I suspect the idea was to introduce him to the Highway Code in order he not take his 'racing' habits onto the country's highways and byways which, let me tell you, bore no logical or rational resemblance to gentlemanly etiquette. If you can't pass the bastard – kill him. As nobody died, the accident later transpired as a tit for tat. Although in truth the misjudgement was mine. Taking my son out to teach him anything was always a big mistake. - - - He wasn't joining. Big time. Very big time as we would come to discover.

The caravan and its contents plus the skip loads of rubbish I had been collecting for the last few years was still burning five days later when the removal man arrived. It was customary to inform the local VFB (the Volunteer Fire Brigade) of an impending burning to negate them being 'called out' on a false alarm, which I did. However the arrival of the removal man followed by the local fire investigator was a cause for a reunion. The last time they had met had been a refinery fire at Milford Haven a few years previously. Or so they said.

"Black. Sloeblack. Crowblack. Black - - isn't it?" said the fireman as he approached removing his fire-fighting helmet which for some reason he had donned as he got out of his vehicle. Perhaps he thought I couldn't read the bi-lingual writing emblazoned across the breadth of the car's metal exterior. "Yes it is. But there's no fish-bobbin' in amongst it." I replied. The man's eyes widened. "Duw, duw. I see you'se familiar with the 'Bard'. There's lovely isn't it." The man peered closer. "Nicely confined though. That's lovely. Just checking you see. Black smoke you see. Not good black smoke. Chemicals isn't it." I smiled. One does. I find it helps. "Bottom of the pile. There must have been a couple of old tyres under all the crap. Unavoidable I'm afraid." He bowed to replace his helmet. "Unavoidable. Yes. So many unavoidables'. We'se finds them all the time. So many unavoidable fires we keep turning out to. You would think there should be a law against it wouldn't you?" I shrugged and extended the smile. "Can't do this one -." The voice of the removal man reached my ears from inside the porch. "It's the trees. Too much overhang all along the lane. Scratch the van to bits. Can't be done. Get them trimmed back and it wouldn't be a problem. But as it is -. Sorry." She, who must at least be listened to, standing in the porch, saw my smile fade even from that distance. The local removal man had been asked for a quote four weeks previously and with less than ten days to go before the notice to quit only now tells us he can't do the job because his van might get scratched. I wonder had he thought about his eyes - - . "I know someone who can do that for you bach isn't it." said the fireman, "Good hedge trimmer. Not expensive. Deals in cash. Duw, duw. Do it straight away he could," I watched for a reaction from the removal man as I sensed the Welsh Mafia connection. I remember Braveheart telling me -. "Wheels within wheels sunshine. Nothing happens by coincidence. Not in this valley." I declined the so called generous offer. Nothing in this valley get's done that quickly and immediately is out of the question. Unless of course - - - - it's bent.

Over the period of a week we 'flitted', (a Northern expression to move from one abode to another), with the aid of a hire van and the family. She, who must at least be listened to, had secured a rental in the nearby village large enough for our needs and with a number of large gardens again stuffed full of years of 'deleterious dumping matter'. I was becoming to think I had been drawn to this part of the British mainland in order to cleanse it after a band of marauding rural despoilers had had their way with it. The landlord had felled four or five dozen Leylandii trees some years previously which he then piled up in the centre of the gardens and simply left. Now overgrown with masses of brambles only my best efforts at forming a path all along their circumferences enabled movement around them at all. A trek through the Amazonian jungle would have been easier.

Two of the gardens had been used for constant incineration. Everything from bed springs to car parts and household refuse charred and piled high. Even working on the problem each and every day it would take months to return the gardens to anything of worth. But it was a challenge as my Welsh neighbours liked to say. So were the 'Labours of Hercules' but he was allowed to kill his wife and son and work it off as a penance. All I got was abuse from the neighbours with lighting the odd garden bonfire. But nothing ventured nothing gained as they say.

Fortune smiled in some quarters as we managed to reduced our 'livestock' to a dog and a cat and the boy's pet rat and five horses, the sixth having killed itself charging, for whatever reason, the fence line and lancing itself through on a broken tree-branch. Indeed, the life of a smallholder is never that simple. To ensure the horses would have a reasonable continued existence we gave them away to people we knew, on long term loan, with the proviso of return should their stay at the establishment become, for any reason, untenable. Thus situated we settled down to village life and a tarmac road in constant use with moving traffic as the village served as a 'cut through' between two major highways. Forty five ton pantechnicon wagons and all manner of huge farming machinery trundled through at all hours of the day and night and frequently brought the village to a standstill. A distant and far cry from a rural idyl.

But this was the twenty first century. All manner of things could happen. Throwing caution to the wind and having nothing better to do she, who must at least be listened to, decide to take herself and her voice and wander the world as a 'Holiday Rep', Western Europe and bits of the South. At fifty two years of age (she still looked about thirty to me) she applied and was accepted as a budding 'representative' for the Spanish holiday market and six months summer work on the island of Formentera – a Spanish enclave.

"I've stocked the freezer up -." she announced one blustery morning in the month of March. "I'll see you in October." The taxi was waiting outside. "Oh – and I've left you a cell phone. It's on the kitchen table. My number is in the call section." she added as the front door closed. A what! A cell phone? What the - - ? Perfectly executed – and the taxi moved off. I hated cell phones. She knew my aversion to having a spy-phone about my person. So much so I hadn't the first inkling as to how they worked or how to operate one and as for 'texting' my fingers were just too big and it would have been quicker and easier for me to send off a bloody homing pigeon –. A bloody cell phone? Are you kidding me! -----.

I used that first half-year interlude to bring some order from the chaos of the gardens and to redecorate the whole of the house internally. Which is probably why I ended up in the hospital having chest x-rays and when I discovered, finally, that I didn't have emphysema and never had and that I wasn't going to die prematurely unless I got hit by a bus, which was now a possibility as we now lived on a bus route. In fact, given my present state of health was much more likely. According to my new doctor -. "There's nothing wrong with you lad – (lad, he must have been thirty years younger than me)! You have been over-doing it. Exhaustion -. You're not built to be working twenty hours a day. Ease off a bit." That, at first, didn't seem to ring true. I had always worked nights and days as I deemed necessary since leaving school so -. "You're sixty one years old, not twenty one. Time to cool it." he added for fine measure. "I could prescribe tranquillisers if you think it will help?" Not on your nelly I thought. Pills? I don't do pills. Nicotine I will take as much as you've got. But not pills. – Well you don't know what's in them do yer -! "No thanks I'll stick t' my fags." I replied. A snort of displeasure returned what he thought of that but he made no attempt at any dissuasion. It would have been useless anyway. At my eventual demise I will probably be found trying to cadge a light for my 'dimp' from one of the cleaners in some wayward old folks home. Stop smoking! I had been smoking since I was nine years old. Chest pains or not and with emphysema or not, hell would have to freeze over first. And not to again put too fine a point on it. He was a General Practitioner -. He could still be practicing! Last one was, she of the bloody booze and dachshunds.

'For the want of a nail –.'

It is beginning to look like this will be the century
of the terror wars, the water wars, the climate
wars and the alien wars – the aliens being the
ever evolving viruses. The attack on the 'twin
towers of York', the 'damming of the river Nile'
and the ever present outbreaks of Ebola, Sars,
Murs and Avian flues. 'Oh what a tangled web we
weave when all we ever do is breed, breed, breed.'
The 'elephant in the room' that nobody sees.
Seven billion and rising as the land surfaces shrink
and our demands outstrip the planets natural
resources. Sustainability is a very big word and it
is obvious those that govern can't spell it – what
cowards we continue to breed and idolise!

It was ten years to the day when the knock came
at my door. It seemed to have a familiar rhythm
to it, one I couldn't immediately place. "I've come
to persuade you to come to the next railway
society meeting -? Richard of Whitland complete
with grass-matted dungarees and sweat band
hovered in the aperture. It wasn't a surprise. For
the past few months I had received a number of
telephone calls ostensibly enquiring after my
health and always ending up with the line 'Why
don't you come to a society meeting?' To which I
had always laughed a parting farewell. Richard
and Eleanor, she of the hippie-flower patterned
frock, having served their ban of the usual

statutory ten years exclusion, had arrived back at the railway a few years previously and in the interim no doubt created their own forms of unintentional chaos. There could only be one reason as to why I would wish to venture on to that unholy ground and that was – obstinacy. A very unhealthy tendency of 'not to give in' and, not to put too fine a point on it, I quite liked it. "When is it?" I enquired, my brain racing to come up with an excuse, "Tonight." He gave one of his rare smiles. Bastard. "Er – I don't know. I'll think about it." I replied. "Well quite a few would like you to come." By that he probably meant the two of them. "We'll see - -. Leave it with me." I moved the subject on towards a conclusion. "Tea is about to be served - - -." He nodded knowing full well that was the end of that particular subject –for now.

My return, initiated by she who at least must be listened to with a -, "You won't be happy until you've given the rest of your life to them -," wasn't applauded by all now ensconced therein, not that such was a problem as I didn't know most of them anyway. The railway had followed its usual pattern of 'thru-put' of the curious, the amateurs, the socialisers and the geniuses (those who knew better than anyone else). We are left at this point in time with the enthusiasts, socialisers and the desperate, the geniuses having move on to other unsuspecting projects.

The railway was again losing money with no expectations of reversing the trend. My first impression was simple – "It's had it." Richard allowed his head to wander from side to side. "Er – Yes. It's not too good is it." Good! Good! Here we go again with bloody British understatement. Good! -"I've gone through the figures. They are less than half when I left. The break-even point is fifteen thousand visitors. It's now nine thousand. On top of which you've franchised the catering for peanuts. Done away almost completely with the shop. Buggered up the miniature railway which hasn't run for the last four years and from what I can see of maintenance or any renovation it's not been touched since I left – and you haven't revamp your tickets prices in the last six years - - What the hell do you expect me to do - - for my next miracle?" Richard waited for his head to stop wandering. "Well - - I don't really know -. But something needs doing." I studied the look of abject pain on the man's face. As the only remaining founder member I could see how much it meant to him. "Best thing to do would be to sell it, - someone with money. Put it back into a properly run private company and out of the hands of the dreamers and the vandals. Make it into what it should have been from the outset. Either a proper heritage railway, in which case it needs to be standard gauge, or a proper tourist railway attraction with all weather, all age group facilities. - - This lot is still going where it has always been going - west -to -nowhere!" Richard let go control of his neck again. "So how do we do that then -?" AAArrrrrrgh! No I didn't actually scream, although a good blow-out would have served me well at that precise moment. "You don't -. Because you can't -. Because you made the bloody place constitutionally bankrupt in 1984. It can't be sold. It can only be terminated, like a squashed bug. Without a constitutional change of gargantuan proportions or the company being put into administration the members are stuck with it – come what may. Yes dear boy – another fine mess you've got me into Stanley." A reference to those very early twentieth century comedians Laurel and Hardy. But believe me, in this instance, they really did fit the bill. The 'real enthusiast', the pitiful few, was worked to death – and then greatly abused for their efforts. In my case it didn't matter. To me that was. My enthusiasm came from a desire to 'create' which as long as I was in a position to do so was satisfying my inner needs, money never entered the equation. Eleanor, she of the flower-patterned hippie dress, was of the same mind, whilst the two or three others had that 'railway bent' and just couldn't abide not being around one. We made a 'motley crew' without which the 'project' couldn't function at all. Eleanor attended to the red-tape, the administration of paper-work, of which there was mountain upon mountain. For an operation drawing less than one hundred thousand pounds per annum the 'paper pile' was humungous. Reams and reams and reams. A modern countries

Armed Forces could have operated on less.

My job, as manager, was the overseeing of all the various departments with the exclusion of 'engineering' or in this case everything to do with the operating of the trains. That was in the hands of 'the Responsible Person' a qualified steam engineer conversant with all railway operating rules under the auspices of the 'Railways Inspectorate' and subject to all its regulations. It was a very responsible job and required a person of aptitude and diligence which, at that precise moment and for the last previous years, this railway didn't have. Alcohol seemed to be the problem. A problem the Board of Directors must have known about but chose to ignore, 'responsible persons' being scarcer than hen's teeth and vital for the continuance of operations. Complaints met with silence. It seemed as long as the man could walk upright and didn't constantly fall off the footplate – all was well with the world. – But railway tracks and rolling stock need regular maintenance for commercial purpose and, more importantly, health and safety, as would become blatantly obvious as time went on.

What it was with rural people and their absence of neat, tidy, clean and pleasing to the eye I am at pains to reconcile. My ten years absence must have been the signal for the dumping and discarding in any available space within eyeshot anything that required an effort to dispose of properly.

Again I set to work to bring order from a chaos and at least a perception of loving care as throughout that winter season with wheelbarrow, shovel, paint brush and bleach I transformed, what at first glance represented a rural scrap yard, into what might hopefully get mistaken for a nice 'tourist attraction' or a 'quaint left-over' from the 'age of steam'. I like to think I succeeded. Throwing caution to the wind I employed a local diesel engineer who within days got the miniature railway up and running again – and to hell with backlash which would inevitably come from Engineering or disgruntled 'Board Members'. The tragedy the venue was unlikely to get over had been the earlier years from the turn of the century up until the collapse of the financial markets when the economy was booming and there was money to be made. Now, in 2010, we are diving into a long recession and a constant time of austerity. Money is tight at a time when expenditure, to give a boost, was very much needed and it wasn't there. The first priority is 'exposure' which with a poor location throws up all kinds of problems. The internet could meliorate a good section whilst the old and tested leaflet distributions take care of the rest. It was a start. Furthermore a sensible ticket price which reflected the present day perception and likewise in both cafe and shop now residing in the same building. The 2010 season we broke even. The 2011 season made a small but distinct profit which put a smile on the company's local bank manager's face as it had been decades since the last time such a thing had happened. It was by no means perfect. The lack of proper maintenance was going to prove expensive as buildings, fences, pathways, dangerous trees, culverts, bridges, regulations for disabled access, not to mention all the track and bed, rolling stock and machinery that was in a woeful condition and to cap it all the usual desperate need for volunteers and capable staff. All threatened to push the venue towards inevitable extinction. It wasn't as though any of it had missed my inner-most thinking. It was crazy.

As the 2012 season was coming to an end I had come to a decision. 2013 promised to be no better than the three previous. The meagre profits need only one small disaster which could throw, indeed hurl, everything back to square one in a flash. After all the years previously and now yet again to be worse off than at the projects inception was most definitely not something I was remotely interested in. It was getting make or break time and my patience, after twenty three years of continual attendance (thirty three active in total), was now finally coming to an end.

'Guess which one is me'.

'Mr. Howard Canitbe.'

It had been a very mild and almost pleasant September. We have entered our interim closed period, that which occurred between school half term and following Halloween and the term before Christmas. As usual I was the only person on site. It was rare for volunteers or engineering to attend until the 'punters' returned with their pockets of cash and hordes of wide-eyed children. Today I'm emptying the 'wishing well' which surprisingly was one of the few 'attractions' that actually made a good profit when, from the distance, I heard the rattle of the Judas gate, the main gate being closed to dissuade 'rubber-neckers' and the outline of the 'Glimmer Man' as he wandered down the yard. I should explain at this juncture I was unaware he cosseted such a life as of one deserving of such a title - - - .

He was smallish and thin in stature with a smoothness of pallor and bright twinkling eyes and at a guess in his late thirties. I nodded. Not knowing what to expect.

"I'm looking for the owner." he said, the accent not Welsh and not one I could instantly recognise. "Is he around?" - - Not one of thoroughly modern thinking as he would have asked for 'he or she' or possibly 'they' I thought.

I smiled. One had to. Such a question, in this particular case, could lead to all sorts of complications and more often than not did. "There isn't one." I replied -. "–It's more a case of who doesn't own it -." I could see my reply had confused him. He tried again. "No. I mean who is in charge?" "Today – me." I replied. "Ah – good. My name is Melvin. I own the supermarket in Pentrebonnie. Are you the person who can tell me about the place and make decisions?" The question wasn't unreasonable but I was rather busy and I had little time for question and answer sessions which always lead nowhere and satisfied only the questioner. I had deadlines to meet which required no useless interruptions or delays.

It transpired he was looking for somewhere to open a garden centre and had picked the wide open space of the railway yard as one possibility. The idea had merit and I promise I would take it to the Board of Directors at their next meeting, the upshot of which blossomed three fifteen foot long poly-tunnels, after a clearance of unused ground, and a small but worthwhile rental income for little to no outlay. Where could be the harm -?

The pantechnican's arrived a week before half-term to disgorge more than a thousand trees, shrubs and plants of every description and a small crew of labourers culled from the surrounding hillsides to attend them.

Water and electrical connections to the miniature railway sheds helped to complete the required arrangements and orders placed for leaflets announcing the railways latest attraction with a dozen or more roadside posters giving directions. It seemed the man knew his stuff. A pleasant change to what one was normally used to. There appeared not to be any shortage of money. Could this possibly be the small start of something - useful?

"Humph – humph, humph. By Gad Sir. I quite like the cut of your jib -." Mansell-Jones, the Chief Custodian Trustee was working himself up from the haze of the fact he had fallen asleep, albeit momentarily, during the Board Meeting I had called to discuss future plans for the coming season. Nothing had been said upon my return to the railway regarding he himself having been instrumental in 'throwing me from the bridge' during that last 'purge'. It was though it had never happened. " I – er – I think that Mr – er – what was your first name again -?" "Mervin." Offered the Glimmer Man. "Mervin – yes – hmm. Fine name. I once knew a Mervin – yes. Korea I think. Hmm! Leicester you say. Yes. Family name strikes a bell. Didn't we do business? Cattle fodder? Hmm? Seems familiar. Undercover children's play area? Yes – well. Sounds to have merit. Bouncy castle you say. Yes - -. Good man."

Mervin was full of ideas. His approach to a problem was that there wasn't one. 'How hard can it be?' A favourite response to all and any obstacle. I didn't fully concur having most of my life had to look at the ramifications any change of direction might bring. I quite liked the 'bolt-hole' or 'safety-net' should, as can always happen, the shit hit the fan. Which in my case it had a tendency to do – but then, as the old man had informed the whole world through the pages of the 'Woman's Own' magazine, 'ower youngest lad has alus been a problem'. Thank you father. I'm sure they all needed to know that. Had they have bothered to asked the old lady her response would have been much more succinct – Bloody barmy -! And she would have left it at that. [*I have the greatest of respect for both my parents and their generation born at the end of the Great War and for everything they suffered under. Without doubt the 'Greatest Generation' of the 20th century – and always will be.*]

My costing for the proposed new all-weather play area was around £7 -£8,000. Mervin smiled. "I know where I can get it done for less than half that – not a problem." The Board was impressed. I was sceptical but as always my glass was still half-full. We shall see.

I had worked hard, bloody hard, through the winter of 2012 to make the place as clean, bright and welcoming as it could possibly be.

For once it shone and the new garden centre gave the whole an extra aura of care and friendliness. We were ready for the 2013 Easter opening. All the marketing had been done. Now all we needed was good weather – not too good – we didn't want it to be beach weather. Hordes, hopefully, of tourists lying on beaches for the whole of their stay did nothing for our much further inland attractions.

We opened on the Good Friday, ran two trains and came to a stop. "She's blown a tube." The Chief Engineer explained. "Blown a tube! She's just had her winter maintenance – hasn't she?" My stare at the steaming locomotive standing idle on the yard points had that glint of annoyance. "You can never tell when she's going to blow a tube. It just goes and happens isn't it," he retorted obviously disdainful of my lack of knowledge on the subject. His ignorance of my knowledge, or anyone else's for that matter, was the reason we rarely saw eye to eye. I knew for instance that one of the tubes had a small leak from a previous 'volunteer fun-day' some six weeks previously which he had obviously ignored and passed over in his usual lack of care for the rolling stocks vital attention. "We had better put the diesel on then. I will cancel the next departure time and put the board to two-o-clock." The Chief Engineer passed his hand across his brow and lifted the nib of his bowler hat.

"She's not running." he said. "Starter motor. We have it in pieces. Not looking good- yet." My jaw seized up. I remember thinking. 'You must be fucking joking -.' "Can't you jump start it?" I hissed through clamped teeth. "Jump start! S'not a car bach. Doesn't work that way. Three and a half tons of pure metal isn't it. And you could smash the gears." his eyes widening in stark effrontery. "Duw, duw. We doesn't do that." Possibly not, I thought, but there was most certainly one thing I would like to 'do' and 'smash' that would have given me the utmost satisfaction at that particular moment in time and it wasn't in the form of a locomotive. We have two steam locomotives, three diesel locomotives, none of which are running, a yard full of 'punters', we are fully staffed to ensure the 'Crazy Golf', the new 'Petanque Alley' (that's French Boules to you), the Kid's Playroom, the miniature railway to Pixie Glade and garden centre are primed to go along with everything else and the place is buzzing with energy and now, now our prime attraction, the very reason we are actually in being, the only reason hundreds of pounds are resting in our customers pockets for the spending of - - no longer exists. I did the only right thing possible at that juncture. A smart about turn and I walked away leaving him standing in the middle of the yard still scratching uselessly at his sweat grimed stained forehead. In God's name why oh why did I bother? - - Could anyone tell me - - please!

For the rest of April it was a game of Russian roulette. Spin the wheel. Do we have a running locomotive today? Yes. Good, but will we get through the day before for whatever ridiculous non-sensible reason it becomes unworkable? No. Will you surpass yourself today and inform the next family of expectant passengers that they can actually have a train ride? Er – possibly. Never mind. Scrub railway and change the sign over the gate to 'garden centre with cafe and interesting antique artefacts from a bygone age'. That might possibly placate Mr and Mrs Birmingham who having driven thirty miles for a train ride now discover they can only buy Welsh cakes, a window box plant and for little Johnny, the wide-eyed grandchild, a locomotive that actually works in the form of Thomas the Tank Engine – and friends.

It was the straw that broke the camel's back. In my case possibly straw-bale or a whole harvested field and no, it isn't stupidity. I have a wide stretch of tolerance. Human beings were never meant to be anything other than an imperfection. I know. I am one. But, as with water dripping on the stone, eventually it wears it away. It was time for a decision. Do I go or do I stay? I chose the latter.

 "Tomorrow I close the gates. You can have the keys. I'm gone – done with it." Eleanor looked at me her jaw having dropped somewhere around her lower neck line. "Close the gates – what -!"

'Whatever is planned – forget it.'

The cafe franchiser had given up the struggle to make it pay following the Christmas opening. Mervin, how hard can it be, had taken over the franchise and proven to be first class with his choice of menus and his 'hail hearty well-met' service and the regular rental payments which Eleanor happily scooped up at the end of each month. "Give me a lease. We can run the lot if you want. How hard can it be." he offered eagerly. Eleanor, she of the flowered hippie dress, departed hurriedly to draw-up a suitable rental agreement that would run initially for five years with reviews thereafter. Such a decision would normally have gone before the Board of Directors at the next meeting and probably taken six months to initiate, if at all. I wasn't in the mood to tarry on maybe's. I relented and agreed the end of the month before my departure.

"I could do with you here to look after the railways interests. On a ad hoc basis," said Mervin, giving me that smile. "You know of where everything is and all about the place and someone should look after the shop. – Oh yes and I pay expenses. You could run the railway shop for them, sell the tickets for me. How hard can it be? I can stock the shop properly. Anything of mine you pay me. How hard can it be?" To cut a long story short the company and the trustees agreed to the new arrangements by which Mervin set about revitalising the place for the rest of the year.

The yard was widened nearly doubling its area, the years and years of debris and all manner of unpleasant detritus removed, the engineering/ carriage shed relieved of all its claustrophobic filth making it possible to actually walk' not just up and down' but in all spaces in between and the two derelict caravans hauled out from the undergrowth and burned to avoid any possible contraction of deadly disease. The second caravan blowing up brought about the soon expected arrival of the emergency services who descended bells clanging within minutes of what must have been a possible terrorist attack, as reported by one of the local villagers whose house, he maintained, had moved six inches off its foundations into the air before crashing back down again. "We must have missed a gas bottle under all the crap." explained Mervin, seemingly not at all concerned for the Chief Fire Officers foaming at the mouth. "Missed you say. Missed? We've missed our lunch having this call-out. Caul and brown baps it was too. The boy's look forward to their Wednesday caul so they does. Delicious it is." The Chief Fire Officer calmed down considerably when Mervin offered them Pepperoni panzerotti and a glass of cider each from the cafe and free family train tickets for the coming weekend. Food it seemed had a currency in our neck of the woods. Bribery - - ! Most certainly not. It's called appreciation for our emergency services. - - - Is'n it - -!

The field above the North bank of the railway yard was rarely used, swampy and housing a mass of sharp-pointed reed grasses, the adjoining farmer took little care of the boundary fence. "S,not his problem. Railway regulations isn't it. We are supposed to fence the farmers out, not them fence us in." Richard of Whitland was glad to inform me after the two ponies followed by the four goats had partially demolished it. Today all that I could see were the heads of Mervin's staff popping up and down with cries of "Where the fuck are they?" I was instantly taken back to my childhood and the tale of the 'Fukcawi' tribe of the Serengeti who hailed from the pygmy variety and spent most of their lives wandering aimlessly amongst the tall grasses of that endless plain bouncing up and down continuously crying "Were the Fukcawi. Were the Fukcawi." - - "What are they doing?" I asked, although I'm sure I didn't really want to know. "The Poles got out last night." said Mervin. "Little bastards." - Now I'm not usually slow on the uptake but for a moment that had me flummoxed. Visions of Polish labourers flashed through my mind and the words illegal immigrants or trafficked slaves – not that I wouldn't have put it passed he of few morals. Prior to opening for the season Mervin had decided to add a 'Pet's Zoo' (entrance free with a rail-ticket) to the myriad of attractions whizzing daily through his cunning brain. A good quarter of an acre of scrubland, so far unused, served to house the pens for the captive inhabitants. Rabbits, pigs, ponies, geese, chickens, hamsters, lambs and last but not least ferrets, which Mervin insisted on calling polecats or in this instance - 'poles'. Delightful little creatures and absolutely adorable although on more than one occasion we had to release inquisitive children's fingers from their incisor teeth and in one case from the chin of a screaming, now terrified, nine year old whose mother threatened to 'inform the authorities' regardless of the notice saying 'Do Not Touch The Animals'. She relented when Mervin suggested that, "There were no medicines for stupid although we did have sticking plasters for dumbasses." The hunt continued throughout the afternoon with a prized total of two 'finds' and was called off as darkness descended.

The following morning the ferret pen was full again. It was feeding time as no self-respecting ferret was going to miss out on a free breakfast. "The Poles are back in town. The Poles are back in town." sang Mervin as he headed for the signal box. Mervin had plans for the signal box, presently a small GWR museum, although it wasn't actually in his remit. Not that that seemed to worry him. "How hard can it be?"

Within weeks the signal box, now renamed 'The Rail Snack Box' sprouted a raised wooden terrace with steps up housing six picnic tables and the appropriate royal bunting for the use of.

Internally was a small pizza bar and room to swing a cat. "We will use it to take the rush off the cafe in the high season. Quick meals in the sunshine." he said. I nodded, sagely, as one does. There was only one flaw in his thinking. What 'rush' and which 'sunshine'. We hadn't had a decent summer for years. As for a huge increase in visitor numbers a ten percent increase didn't constitute viability considering the enormous amounts of cash he had been expending to date on the 'project'. Marketing or the lack of was the only answer. Tell them where you are and what you have, otherwise, they're not coming.

"I've got some cartoon costumes. Minions. Fireman Sam, Mr Blobby and Donald Duck. This afternoon we are going around the caravan parks giving out leaflets. That should bring them in." Admittedly it was unusual and would, no doubt, cause quite a stir, but we desperately needed to inform tens of thousands of our bold existence not a few hundred that might remember to come the next day – if we are lucky.

At the outset of Mervin's arrival and his now consequent overall control of the venue I had reminded him of his promise when I said. "You will need to invest at least a quarter of a million pounds over the next couple of years to put the place in order and add attractions to boost the numbers towards a good profitable outcome."

He had assured myself and the Board of Directors that such an amount was already available and wasn't a problem.

And to be truthful it seemed it wasn't. On my own calculations the amount of expenditure after the first twelve months bordered on approximately half that amount. But without a proper marketing strategy and delivery I couldn't see how his mind-set of 'build it and they will come - regardless' - would work? It never had in the past. It's not the bloody pyramids. Word of mouth in these sparsely populated regions was so slow one would have been better grabbing an old carpet and sending Red Indian smoke signals -! However Christmas is approaching and Mervin's plans are really something to behold. Tomorrow is another day. How hard can it be?

The 'Santa's Grotto' marquee and stuffed reindeer were in place at 'Santa's Halt'. Fifty new Christmas trees with star-lights adorned the half mile miniature track and 'choose your own present' stacked in 'Santa's Post-office where parents delighted in mince pies and sherry. Centre yard a new all-weather rotunda awaited fitting out with Christmas toys, drinks and snacks - - when the storm hit. 'Cyclone Dick' sorry 'Dirk' blew in on the Sunday, stayed for two days, then blew out again taking half of Santa's marquee, the newly constructed rotunda, uprooted two dozen of the newly planted Christmas trees and all the external Christmas decorations - - - as it left .

Yes. That's just how hard it can be – and quite often is. Welcome to the world of 'hospitality' my friends and the best laid plans of mice and men.

"Duw. Duw. That's a bit of a blow isn't it?" The Chief Engineer tried to look sympathetic, as does the jackal who lost his kill to the lion who then lost it to the human poachers, "Bit of a mess now isn't it?" The Chief Engineer had been fired, begged forgiveness vowing he would change and had been reinstated on a trial run, but fully aware Mervin had other plans in the pipeline. The cost financially was considerable by the railways standards which didn't seem to faze Mervin one little bit as the storm returned again and again over the holiday period each time creating havoc in its wake. The four plus thousand visitors dwindled to a fraction of around one and a half thousand of the sturdier types hell-bent on having a good Christmas come hell or high water which, considering the depth of water in 'Santa's Grotto', was considerable for most of the time.

I surveyed the damage with a critical eye. All could be overcome and there was no doubt with three months to go before the opening of the next season our 'Glimmer-man' had the wherewithal to produce a good-quality product by then – . I tried again to convince him regarding the venue's lack of marketing. Leaflets. Half a million. Swamp the region. Tell them 'we are here'. What could go wrong? How hard could it really, really be?

True to form, her ten year attendance coming up, Eleanor, she of the flower-patterned dress, took her spanner and hurled it into the machinery. Mervin rarely got angry. Today he's livid. Eleanor only ever ventured down for half an hour each day to pocket the shop takings and extract the pertinent postage from the mail box on the gate outside. Today Mervin's brother, Saint Peter of Leicester, as he was known, had some disturbing news. Someone had 'hacked' their Christmas account and removed some of the data. No monies were missing but who had been given the passwords to enable such an action? Being within earshot my heart sank. Here we go again.

Saint Peter was the goose laying the golden egg. Regardless of Mervin's assertions I knew full well that no monies arrived at the railway without his 'holinesses' sanction. Pete pulled the purse strings. Merv ran the show. Everyone was happy - if this was kept just so-. Interference from outsiders would not be brooked. Hacking Pete's accounts was beyond being a cardinal sin – it was a definite no ,no. Today the 'tap' was being turned off. Saint Peter had had more than enough and without a regular input of money to pay the wages, over and above our own meagre income, the 'project' would be inevitably lost. "You tell that bitch to stay away." Mervin growled on my approach. "If she comes here again I'll personally kick her over the bloody gate."

He was well within his rights of course although relations between the two of them had been going from bad to worse for the last six months, something I had warned her about but to which she had paid scant attention. Eleanor had always been her own 'master'. As a founder member she considered hers to be an inalienable right to direct the railway in whatever course of action she saw fit and against 'all-comers' regardless of the Board of Directors (whom she considered idiots) wishes.

And so began the 2014 season with the addition of another large marquee for go-cart racing and an additional poly-tunnel housing tropical plants. Somehow the wages were being paid and nothing seemed to halt Mervin's grabbing lust for personal enjoyment and a forthcoming success. But without Saint Peter and his bountiful baskets (he no longer visited as he had previously) I really was at a loss to understand how things could carry on.

It was the Railway's Inspectorate's five yearly inspection. A two day visit to ensure all health and safety regulations were in place and that the railway stock, tracks, operatives and appropriate paperwork were in good order and all were suitably qualified for the safe operation of the passenger hauling of trains – albeit at a maximum of ten miles an hour.

I knew it wasn't up to its proper potential. But it was safe – as all things go.

To Hell And Back.

Apart from one very short interlude, she who must be at least listened to, and myself, had never been in a commercial situation where we had worked closely together. These last few years at the small tourist railway had changed all that. For the most part I took care of the miniature railway, herself, the ticket office and railway shop. Unsurprisingly it worked out well. At least there was harmony in the commercial side of things for once as we both got on well with Mervin and his family without deference having to be paid in our capacities of both volunteer and employee at one and the same time. She, who must at least be listened to, had been years in the service industries, in one form or another, and knew just how to handle any type of customer who thought they were being attended to by less than common 'serfs'.

"I think we are entitled to a rebate. There are eight of us and it cost forty pounds for a forty minute train ride – a pound a minute." said the father of the Jewish family whose children were at that moment running amok in amongst the tidy shelving of the railway shop. "I split the family into a family ticket and four extra children and reduced the total by ten percent – as we negotiated." replied the wife.

"It's an all-day ticket which entitles you to another free ride on the big train and a free ride on the miniature train. There are 'eight' of you Sir." The man fumbled in his open wallet, probably to remove the dust that had settled therein or remove any dead chrysalises. "And there was no water in the Celtic Leet." he growled. The wife, not one to be flustered, questioningly cocked her head to one side. "No water in the 'leet'"? "Barely. Hardly a trickle. We had to walk right down to it to see anything -!" he snapped irritably. The wife handed him back the tickets. "Perhaps if you have a word with your 'man'," - she indicated towards the ceiling ,-" he could do something about that before you take another of your free train rides. If you're nice enough he might throw in an earthquake or two whilst he's at it. Just to give you that little extra bit of holiday excitement. - - Next please - -." Time and the small queue that had formed behind the Jewish couple wait for no man – especially not this one. The wife glanced into the shop area where devastation was still taking place as the man's children picked up everything in sight and dropped it wherever it might fall – which was everywhere. This could turn out to be a very annoying, if not a frustrating, afternoon. But it was - 'all in a day's work for the commonly hard-pressed hospitality and service industry. 'I thank you Sir – Sincerely'.

Cutting a long and boring story short we advanced the season ever hopeful with good grace.

"Well that's yet another fine mess you've got me in to Stanley -." Why Mervin was looking at me and not towards the advice I had given him over the past eighteen months I couldn't imagine. Admittedly they were 'my people'. I had advised him to remove them at the onset of his project. He, on the other hand, said he could manage them. Obviously such had not been the case.

The first mile of track was condemned. In places out of gauge and too many unsuitable sleepers. Laid in 1983 of second-hand materials and lacking proper maintenance for the last ten years it came as no surprise to me that after thirty years the 'Railway Inspector' was no longer impressed (although in truth it had been in a similar condition on the previous inspections which had then 'passed muster'). Likewise the second mile of track, although repairs could bring it into line, which having been laid on a shale shelf again came as no surprise. 'Operations suspended' until repairs carried out and the whole lot re-inspected.

"Middle of fucking July -! What fucking good will that be -?" Mervin stomped around the cafe. Which was not a good idea considering the fragile condition of the uneven wooden flooring. "And that bitch." he was referring to Eleanor, she of the recent wanton ways, "- who does nothing but moan about the bloody rent whose agreement says quite specifically that the railway's assets are in good order and can be relied upon at all times.

What 'times' did she mean? When it suits her brain-dead responsible person who spends half his time flopping around pissed out of his head?" Ooops! I looked for a suitable distraction, today was, I could tell, not going to be a good day - -.

"Rip the fucking lot up." Mervin was meaning the first mile of track. No half measures then. Dispense with the problem and relay new rail and sleepers. It seemed like a good idea at the time. The following week two wagon loads of new sleepers arrived. - - -How hard can it be.

Meanwhile. The 'Land-train' arrived. Resplendent with its three gaily painted carriages (hay-trailers) and made-up steam engine (in essence a tractor with added additions) for the conveyance of rail-passengers down the empty track-bed. I know I shouldn't but the urge just overcame me. "Er – did you get the recordings?" Mervin looked at me blankly. "The recordings, you know. The audio tapes and PA system with the clickety-clack and train whistle sounds to go with it?" Sarcasm was one of Mervin's regular weapons. He smiled. "Touché Atlas lad, touché. - - Assehole - - ." I grinned. Well what else could I do. We are all well on our way to Disneyland, especially with this celebrated Pied Piper in the lead. Whatever next -?

The telephone call came after the Bank Holiday. Eleanor, she of more wonton ways, was furious.

"He's chopping the forest down!" From my vantage point on the cattle-dock I was observing the third forestry wagon trundle from under the bridge loaded down with its load of Neta pine. "Yes. I know." I replied. "Well he can't." she responded indignantly. I watched the wagon leave the yard. "Well he looks to be doing a pretty good job of it to me." I quipped. "That's the third wagon load today." "Well stop him. Lie down in front of the wagons if you have to – but stop him." she shrieked.

Mervin had employed a local contractor to remove the forestry. Each man at least six foot thirteen inches tall and nearly that wide. I was going to stop him? Methinks not. Not that I needed to. "We sold him the forestry and it has a felling order on it -. What am I supposed to do? He has every right to do with it as he pleases, apart from set fire to it - - and I wouldn't put that passed him if you try to interfere – yet again?"

It transpired the full monies for the sale had not been forthcoming. The agreement however did not state work couldn't start after half the monies had been paid, a common practice in these parts, which they had. Yet another small detail of which the Board of Directors were unaware. Meanwhile Mervin was extracting his pounds of flesh from wherever his talents could acquire them - and so the wagons trundled on - as did my lingering doubts of earlier in the season. They didn't bode well.

Relaying the track in time for the forthcoming 'Santa Specials' was to begin at the start of October. Eleanor, she of the flower-patterned frock and more recently wanton ways, has departed for the third time. This time with a life-time ban and to never darken the railways creaking point-levers ever again. The 'sin' of 'thinking for oneself' and 'keeping dark secrets' had not gone down well with either the Board or the Custodian Trustees who operated on the well tried and tested theory that 'a man's word is his bond' and could not deviate from that no matter what. A laudable sentiment but hardly applicable in the 21st century. As Company Secretary her actions should have been at the behest of the company and not solely undertaken clandestinely, rightly or wrongly. "Throw her under the wagons-." ordered the Chief Trustee. One has to give him his due. He loved his feudal lord of the manor role – in fact he revelled in it. It seemed a week couldn't pass without him sacking some poor peasant somewhere, even when they were totally innocent.

The second week of October everyone arrived bright and early. Today the new rail should arrive. It didn't - and neither did Mervin. Nor the next day or the next. In fact never again. The 'Glimmer Man' had jumped ship. Without a by your leave or even a telephone call. Gone. Auf Wiedersehen Pet. Only he wasn't my 'pet'. Simply a product of our times. A confidence trickster? Actually no. A dreamer with a glib tongue? Yes. Most certainly.

I tendered my resignation along with all the other members of the Board as it was the right thing to do. Collectively we should have seen it coming and tried harder to avoid the final embarrassment of Mervin's debts, which would by now have been considerable, and regaining the trust of our own block of local creditors. The Trustees asked for me to 'stay on' as 'temporary manager' to which I agreed providing it be no more than to the end of the month. Meanwhile the search went out for that 'someone' crazy enough to replace me. Fear not dear reader for there is always one – somewhere. Within a few days he appeared. Yet another ex-manager from ten years previously (the time of my first casting-out) willing again to take on board the 'Mission Impossible' and spend his time trying at what was and always had been a very 'trying' establishment. I wished him well with a parting piece of advice which ran – 'remove any leftovers and don't let any of the old gang anywhere near the place'. In addition – 'try to dump the shackles of the original constitution' – that way you might just stand a slender chance of success.

I like to believe he understood my sincerity as he bent to the task. The 'project' was a good idea but completely decimated by 'best of intentions', a lack of commercial know-how, a gross under funding and a bankrupt constitution. Hellan Railway lived up to its name although 'Hell and Back' may well have been far more appropriate. All things carefully and soundly considered.

I returned to my house and gardens in the village to contemplate my navel, which had remarkably grown a miniscule paunch over the past five years. The bathroom scales didn't lie. They just refused as always to register my presence. Had they been automated with digital message it would have read, 'Try putting your whole body on the foot pad before reading off the weigh scale'. I was trying for nine stone. One of these days I will surprise myself – yea – pigs will fly. Only if they line my coffin with rocks.

"It's time you retired properly," said she who must at least be listened to. "This is the third time. And that means no more daft schemes." She was right of course. First at thirty seven years old then at fifty-six years and now at seventy. I hadn't looked at the gardens in the past five years and that grape vine I discovered in the past was by now attempting to escape into next-doors village pub's car-park. Not only that but all the grape bunches were being snaffled and devoured by serenading late-night drunks and outsider revellers. - - The light came on. Back to the home-made wine which in years gone by I had produced regularly in the many tens of gallons. Where's my grape press? "Hey up lass. How clean is them there feet er yours?" There's no doubt about it. Wives come in very handy every now and then. Splendid idea. And it keeps the super-market bill down. Where's my grape-snips? "Hey up woman. Where's tha' gone now - - - ?"

Final Deliberations.

This is, by necessity, a potted version of my life in Wales and lacks a wide multitude of events and discoveries that happened in-between those years. Ower Deliberations cannot be completed without a personal and honest appraisal of a life well lived and of the past and a possible future for those I leave behind. I was born in a time of a World at War and of a dying Empire. Our early learning's all geared to a glorious past and of a glorious future. Both were a lie. Glorious only in the minds of the safe well-heeled academic whose hands were never soiled with the blood and the gore and whose eyes were closed to the 'disciplines' exacted by the 'Masters'. For the ordinary man in the street, War and Empire mattered little. Food, shelter and a future were all he craved but which to obtain he must suffer whatever outrage the 'State' decidedly imposed. The years since that austere youthful experience (see – the Ower Darkling series) have been sewn with struggles brought on by nature and nurture in equal measure. A decision, around about eleven years old, has always led me towards my own self-satisfaction. The cost has often been great, but happiness is an inner decision which only blossoms at the expense of all else. Money – you can keep it. It really is 'the root and branch of all evils'.

To do without it and the power and control it will bring means settling for less at all times – but it does mean more time for the things that really matter in the long run. Companionship, in whatever form, and all it can bring runs foremost. No man is an island. Unless of course he's insane to begin with. However man is a beast, an animal with an evolved brain. Capable of all kinds of obscenities from simple domestic or child abuse to genocide on an unimaginable scale. Granddad Sam once said, shortly after the end of 'his' second world war, 'Trust in no-one lad only tha self. Un then, only half trust thesen.' Meaning of course that we ourselves are not fully in control of our own actions at times and thus must be continuously self-vigilant, less we succumb to the inner beast and the ills of the world around us. He was a good man who died long before his allotted time doing a good turn for a neighbour – after two world wars, the General Strike and the poverty that followed the Wall St crash and no automatic Welfare State or National Health Service – how's that for a kick in the teeth. "Justice - - !" scowled miserable Grandma, she who begat my mother, "Tha's ont wrong planet lad." - - She could have scowled for England that one. I don't remember ever having seen her smile – not once in the thirty odd years I knew her. But then – she never had the freedom to choose her life like we had. The ending of the Second World War brought about that sea-change which led to the 'glorious nineteen sixties' a decade we have paid for ever since but which on balance no-one could have afforded to miss. The decades since have been a melange of an island race trying to discover its new role in the greater scale of things and for the most part failing somewhat miserably. Courageous we may be. Big-hearted we are not – other than in times of dire national emergency and 'needs must'.

Which brings me full circle and lands us the deadly disease that swings in on the silent, invisible wings of a cruel parasitic virus, born from a world of ongoing human crass stupidity and carelessness.

Covid 19 or as some would have it 'the Chinese Flu'. It no more deserves that designation as does a previous flu pandemic following the Great War of 1914-1918 and named the Spanish Flu as neither may have sprung from either of those two much maligned countries. However it is without doubt a product of man's interference with the natural order of things. In a world whose nature is rapidly changing, due to man's actions, where weather patterns despoil the lands, where food can no longer be grown, where populations continue to explode and where man's ingenuity can no longer keep pace with a downward slide towards our species own demise, for billions it does not bode well. The human species may well survive for millennia to come but never again will it live as free a spirit as it does today. The 21st century will bring the terror wars, the water wars and the virus wars and the worst war of all – our climate.

Control and order will become the accepted norm as those that are not 'culled' are allowed to survive for the needs of balance and for the satisfaction of a future existing. On the planet we call 'Earth' it cannot come to pass in any other way. Such is man's inherent nature and quest for self-survival – at all costs – to a point.

To my children (who know me too well) and my grandchildren who know of my existence I say. "Pick the bones out of that. Just ensure they are not your bones that are being picked out by someone else." To the rest of mankind this is just simply a - 'Warning from History'. Heed it well.

'Here endeth the lesson -!'

That is the end of my story. I sincerely hope I haven't bored you too much. By necessity it has been a condensed version. I could have filled another three volumes – but would I have lived that long? At the beginning, a list of the previous books in the series and following on here for the devotee of the 'war genre', a further list of WW2 operations of lesser known facts. Please feel free to enjoy.

For now 'fair fortune' to you all. May your lives be as full and as fortunate as mine has been and may 'your' God (I don't have one – unless it was in the form of the old lady – my mother) go with you.

Atlas D'four 2021.

Other Books by Atlas D'four.

Published by UkUnpublished in 2010.

Available now through Amazon/Kindle in

e-book and paperback.

'SCRIPTS ON BLACK' Series. (WW2 non-fiction).

   (Chronological Order ref: date line).

Black Venge'nce   978-1-84944-044-8

Originally published by Blackie & Co.

ISBN 1-904986-10-2- now out of print.

Black Despair   978-1-84944-045-5

Black Hors' d' oeuvres   978-1-84944-046-2

Black Dawn   978-1-84944-047-9

Black Masquerade   978-1-84944-048-6

Black Princes   978-1-84944-049-3

Black Shark   978-1-84944-050-9

Black Dove   978-1-84944-051-6

Black Dust   978-1-84944-052-3

BlackJack (Counter factual)   978-1-84944-053-0

   Atlas D'four AKA. Raymond Sanderson. 2021.